UNDERSTANDING SUICIDE

Every year millions of people are touched
by suicide. Some attempt to take their own
lives; others are the friends and families of
suicide victims. Every case brings deep
internal grief, unresolved doubts, and
questions:

What happened?
Whose fault is it?
What do we do now?

After centuries of misinformation, we have
more myths than facts about self-
destruction. This book clears up the
confusion and helps people face the
tragedy. It offers practical steps and
spiritual comfort for those who are
despondent and thinking of suicide ... ways
to rebuild their lives and discover new hope
for tomorrow.

UNDERSTANDING

Suicide

WILLIAM L. COLEMAN

David C. Cook Publishing Co.
ELGIN, ILLINOIS—WESTON, ONTARIO

Old Testament scripture quotations are from The Living Bible.
New Testament scripture quotations are from the New International Version.

Published by David C. Cook Publishing Co., 850 N. Grove Ave.,
Elgin, IL 60120
Printed in the United States of America
ISBN: 0-89191-186-3
LC 79-51742
Cover Design by Kurt Dietsch

CONTENTS

Introduction   *9*

PART ONE
FACING THE TRAGEDY   *11*
1   Why Did It Happen?   *13*
2   Why Do They Whisper?   *21*
3   From God's Perspective   *28*
4   Was It My Fault?   *35*
5   Is Suicide Insanity?   *43*
6   We Have a Lot in Common   *50*

PART TWO
FACTS ABOUT SUICIDE   *57*
7   A Look at the Facts   *59*
8   How People Kill Themselves
    without Suicide   *68*
9   The Youth Epidemic   *76*
10   Stalking the Aged   *82*
11   Different Types of Suicide   *89*

PART THREE
THE POTENTIAL SUICIDE   *97*
12   How Can We Tell?   *99*
13   How Can I Get Help for Him?   *109*
14   After the Attempt   *119*
15   The Role of the Minister   *126*

PART FOUR
WHERE TO GO FROM HERE   *133*
16   How Do I Handle My Feelings?   *135*
17   What about the Children?   *142*
18   Do I Need Professional Help?   *149*
19   Rebuilding My Life   *156*
20   There Is Hope for Tomorrow   *162*
    Bibliography   *171*

Acknowledgments

People were generous with their time and feelings. Many affected by suicide were willing to talk and share. I hope their experiences will help lessen the burdens for thousands more.

I owe a special thanks to the people of Aurora, Nebraska: the ministers, library staff, insurance agents, funeral director, a lawyer, a court clerk, a banker, and the person on the street. They were helpful and encouraging. And they patiently answered some of the strangest questions imaginable.

Zandee Nelson was a big help in the early days when I wondered if the project was worth a try.

Chaplain George Updegrove ironed out important questions about alcoholism and self-destruction.

Dr. Paul Welter, counseling psychologist at Kearney State College, performed the ultimate service. He spent long hours going over the manuscript and correcting it. He could not smooth out all my rough spots, but he tried.

The personal stories have been changed enough to protect the individuals' privacy.

IT'S GOOD TO BE ALIVE

This is a book of hope, dedicated to a bright and beautiful tomorrow. It is aimed at lifting people out of despair and giving them the chance to live again.

Every year millions have their lives gutted by the terror of suicide. The attempter, the contemplator, and the survivors are all left in a deep daze. What happened? Whose fault is it? Are we crazy? What do we do now? Their minds whirl in an endless current spiraling downward.

Christians face the shadows of suicide with special confusion. Where was God in the middle of this disaster? Do suicide victims go to heaven? These are problems that strike at the heart of Christian faith and love.

The need is for someone who can help. A concerned person who will listen, field questions, and offer a few suggestions. This book would like to be that friend. It can't answer all the questions or solve each complicated problem. But it's a start. When coupled with a good counselor, the injured person may find his life taking on vitality again.

After centuries of misinformation, there are more myths than facts circulating about self-destruction. This volume aims at helping to clear up the confusion. Hopefully, it can make a difference in your life and in the lives of those you touch.

PART ONE
FACING THE TRAGEDY

ONE

WHY DID
IT HAPPEN?

FEW THINGS TOUCH LIFE with such horror as the act of suicide. Death by cancer or accident carries its own form of agony. But self-destruction tears the survivor apart as little else can.

Those who knew and loved the suicide victim often think he chose to die rather than stay with them. He probably did not feel that way and may have had a totally unrelated reason for his action. Those who are left, however, usually feel strongly rejected. Whether he completed or just attempted suicide, his action has wounded others severely in both heart and mind, leaving them confused, self-incriminated, and filled with despair.

The primary question of all survivors, and the

most difficult to answer, is "Why did it happen?" It would be easy to speculate, give some intriguing statistics, and mechanically place the person into a category; but people are more complicated than that. The fact that a certain percentage of people commit suicide in May and June or the fact that the rate among college students has tripled does not answer the question.

We are talking about a person, not a crop yield or an eclipse we try to predict. In our eagerness for an answer, we grasp for a simplistic solution: He did it because he was in debt or because she called off their engagement.

In reality, suicides are usually caused by many factors that have accumulated over a period of years and finally consummate at one point. In all probability, the person who committed the act was not fully aware of why he did it.

Most of our actions are caused by two, five, thirteen, or thirty reasons, some subtle and forgotten, others current and sharp. Although many factors contribute to the decisions we make, that resulting action is not irresistible. Our goal is to hold on to the power to choose.

Later we will discuss other types of suicide, but for the moment let us confine ourselves to what we might call the desperate suicide: He turned to suicide because he saw no alternative and felt he had to do something. In most cases, the desperate suicide began with inner psychological disturbances. Problems smoldered for many years, occasionally flaring up into a blaze. But for a long time, the potential for fire was internal.

One lady wrote an article for *Reader's Digest* in which she discussed her teenage daughter's attempted suicide. The girl was seemingly an ideal student and child; her parents had no inkling she was suffering from any serious conflicts. But when she was lying on a hospital bed in a semiconscious state, she spewed out long tirades of hate and vulgarity. Her placid nice-girl image was only a cover for a seething pot of hostility that boiled inside. Sometimes the individual himself cannot calculate what is actually going on inside; much less can an onlooker be sure of the emotional state of another person.

A famous apparent suicide of this generation was the highly successful author Ernest Hemingway. Many people dream of having his ability, his adventures, and even some of his escapades; nevertheless, there came a time when some of his external situations started to go sour and ignited his internal conflicts. The critics had begun to denounce his newest writings. Hemingway focused his attention rigidly on these setbacks, ignored his triumphs, and after a period of serious depression, took a rifle and ended his life.

A person's internal or psychological structure can weaken, despite valiant efforts to resist. Sometimes that one last straw causes an individual to buckle under the strain. Consequently, it becomes doubly difficult to answer the question "Why?" If we do not understand the victim's inner struggles, we probably will never find the solution. We have to face the fact that we may have had a close friend or lover whom we really didn't understand.

A teenage girl had placed her hopes high on getting a new dress for a graduation party. Through a series of circumstances she was denied the dress and consequently took an overdose. Was she spoiled? Was she insane? Was she merely throwing a tantrum? Or had she fought many battles in her mind and could fight no more? Finally she merely laid down her arms and surrendered.

We must keep in mind that life holds innumerable variables for all of us. We follow no set blueprint. We can say, however, of those who have committed or attempted suicide, certain internal conflicts seem to be most prevalent.

Dr. Edwin Shneidman, UCLA professor of thanatology, may be the leading authority in America today on suicide. He states a primary cause may be psychological scars from childhood. While the past cannot serve as a catchall to explain each of life's problems, a poor relationship with one's parent or a physical handicap can help distort a person's view of himself. Consequently, the victim may have carried a burden over which he never gained adequate control.

The potential suicide also may have an extremely low estimate of himself. He believes he is incompetent. He has most likely felt this way for some time. Therefore, when life starts to change for him, and especially if it changes abruptly, he feels incapable of handling the situation. He loses his job and is afraid he can't get another one. He graduates and feels unable to enter a new phase of life. He is flooded with a sizable debt and doubts his ability to get it paid. Faberow has written that this type of person is easily given to despair because he doubts his prospects for coping.

A third primary factor may be a seething hostility or aggression. The individual possibly has never lifted a hand against anyone or said an ill word. Still he may feel strongly against a person, an institution, or a situation. Whatever else suicide may be, it is an aggressive act. Often because he is unable or unwilling to take out his hostility on someone else, he eventually turns his aggression upon himself. Dr. Karl Menninger, in his book *Man Against Himself*, said of all the suicides he had investigated, he never found one that did not include suppressed aggression.

Naturally, there are many other emotions that accompany this crisis, such as guilt, depression, and vengeance. Nevertheless, the three we have mentioned—childhood disturbance, incompetence, and aggression—are the basic ingredients that exist in the desperate suicide.

Some people may object at this point and say, "To some extent at least two of these three are true of all of us." Precisely. That is why most people consider suicide at some time in their lives. They may not actually plan it out, but they have at least briefly considered it as an alternative.

These conditions exist with varying intensity in each of us. If over a long period of time they are allowed to maintain a certain level, an individual may be a prime target for some sort of explosion.

Imagine the consequences of continuous failure. A young boy grows up with repeated rejection. He does not do well in school but gets promoted anyway. With each grade he gets further behind. His attention turns to sports in hopes of finding some satisfaction. Each athletic endeavor is a disaster. He cannot look at anything and say, "I do this well." Because he does not do well, he starts to dislike himself. The people around him also begin to put themselves at a distance from the confused child. Later, when his explosive family breaks up, he does not have a chance. His life is like an endless earthquake. Nothing seems secure. With this type of foundation, he may be a prime candidate for suicide.

We remember vividly the final battle the suicide victim lost, either because he attempted or completed the act. What few of us can appreciate is how many similar campaigns he fought and won. Almost no one commits suicide as the result of a single impulse. He has been surrounded before by what seemed like insurmountable odds. He has wanted to quit and just bail out, and yet he has remained. Then a combination of circumstances entrench themselves around him. For some mysterious reason he can cope no longer.

We try to discuss the incident in terms of cowardice or courage. These two emotion-packed terms do not apply and only cloud the real issue. In fact, the victim found himself in a complex situation and saw no other reasonable way out. Feeling trapped, he destroyed himself. As faulty as his logic may have been, he saw himself as the lone soldier surrounded by the ravaging enemy. Though he wanted to live, he saw no alternative but to end it.

The circumstances that finally ignite the explosion may vary considerably. One study found that victims' problems were usually one of three seemingly large obstacles: money, health, and conflicts with relatives. No such pattern or magical number need to be present, but for most suicides, problems do seem to come in groups and consequently swamp the person.

When many problems march in, most of us are set back for a jolt. After the initial shock, however, many of us will set out to make plans to correct the situation. The person who feels completely incompetent finds it more difficult to regroup his resources. He feels inadequate and lacks the resilience to snap back. Unable to cope head-on, and distrusting his ability to solve the problem, he feels hopeless. There is no way out. He believes he has no acceptable alternative. Consequently, he turns to the only way he believes is available. It is this feeling of hopelessness that finally brings him to the edge.

One gentleman, facing death and deeply confused, put it as well as anyone when he said, "I want to die, but only for a little while." When most people come to this brink, their feelings are just as divided. They want to die, and yet they want to live.

The old cliche that people who talk about killing themselves never really do it is far from accurate. Of every ten people who commit suicide, eight give some form of ample warning. Most people attempt suicide in a setting where they might be found and rescued. If anything is characteristic of them as a group, it is their desire to live.

Even the famous kamikaze pilots had trouble killing themselves. One survivor, writing of his ambivalence, said he wanted to die for his country, but he desperately hoped to live. For him, it was not a quiet resolve to end his life.

Dr. Shneidman has written that the suicidal person terribly wants to live. Every suicide is essentially a serious cry for help.

Prior to the tragic step, the person moves into a cloud and his judgment becomes hazy. In a calmer, more deliberate time, he could reason himself out of it. But the cloud's density is overwhelming. If he has lost sleep and has not eaten, his condition is even worse. This is the reason why many people attempt suicide in the early hours of the morning or after a sleepless night.

We need to remember that the suicide victim did not turn against his own life because the car broke down or because he had to cancel the summer vacation. It was not his failure to keep an appointment or because he lost his job. Rather, many things contributed. One day when he felt he could handle no more, one extra thing came along—maybe ever so small—and he did not think he could hold on any longer.

TWO

WHY DO
THEY WHISPER?

THE STORE CLERK WAS TELLING ME a tragic account. A man in his early twenties had recently died and left his new wife stunned. After hearing some of the details, I asked the natural question, "What caused the young man's death?"

The clerk looked quickly to the left, then to the right. He leaned forward and whispered cautiously, "Suicide."

It is no great surprise that the man whispered; most people do. It is evident that we consider suicide a special problem. We don't whisper *emphysema, coronary,* or *stroke,* and we no longer whisper *cancer.* But the stigma long associated with suicide casts shadowy suspicions on the victim. It even raises doubts about his family.

Fortunately, we may be entering a new era in which suicide is no longer considered an act of cowardice or lunacy . . . a day when we realize the most loving wife in the world could not have stopped this tragedy . . . a time when children may realize their father loved them deeply, but could find no escape from this fatal step.

As the lid is lifted, and people accept suicide as a natural problem to be dealt with, many potential victims, families, and friends can be helped. Then people may be more willing to seek assistance to work out their stress before it explodes.

Part of this solution is coming from leaders who have stopped whispering. Literature is now being printed in avalanche proportions. Major cities are now opening Suicide Prevention Centers. These calculate nine out of ten callers are serious, and they believe great numbers are being helped.

Another source that will aid significantly is the raised voice of Christian churches. Many of the issues at stake are basically theological questions about guilt and worthlessness, faith, eternity, and God's acceptance. These ultimate questions can best be answered by ministers teaching God's love from the Scriptures.

Dr. Karl Menninger in *Whatever Became of Sin?* writes that the clergy are in enviable positions when it comes to counseling. In no other profession can one person give an hour of personal guidance to a hundred or a thousand people each week. Most ministers have some very helpful attitudes and suggestions for families facing such difficulties, and laymen should indicate their interest in hearing more on the subject.

Paul described God's interest in people being able to control their minds. He wants to assist every person in keeping a good, healthy balance instead of becoming overwhelmed by problems. "For God did not give us a spirit of timidity, but a spirit of power, of love and of self-discipline" (2 Tim. 1: 7). Pastors can build on such a foundation in their counseling.

In order to understand and combat the present hush, we need to consider how we got our attitudes. Societies have differed over the centuries in approval, toleration, and condemnation of suicide. The ancient philosophers at least three centuries before Christ denounced it. Socrates forbade it on the grounds it remained God's prerogative alone to call men to himself. Any attempt to short-circuit the process was a grave mistake. Interestingly, Socrates himself was later forced to take his own life.

Other cultures, however, not only considered suicide acceptable but, in some cases, preferable. For centuries, Hindu women threw themselves on their husbands' funeral fires. They did this of their own will, even though social pressure doubtless had some influence, due to the difficulty a widow would have in providing for herself.

At the turn of the twentieth century, someone took a survey in parts of China and discovered a startlingly high rate of self-destruction. If the statistics were true across the country, half a million

Chinese were killing themselves every year. This meant that 1 out of every 800 people killed himself each year (compared to 1 out of 8,850 in the United States during the same years).

Our concepts of eternity or heaven seem to be a major factor in our attitude toward suicide. The Judeo-Christian doctrine has stressed that only God has the right to extinguish a human life. This teaching is based on passages such as Job 1:21, "Naked I came from my mother's womb, and naked shall I return; the Lord gave, and the Lord has taken away; blessed be the name of the Lord."

On the other hand, some oriental and more ascetic disciplines consider the present life a shackle. The sooner one could escape these chains and move to a higher existence, the better. Consequently, many Buddhist monks sacrificed themselves on the ritual fires. Some would eat particularly waxy or fatty foods so they would burn better. This attitude explains some of the actions of monks who burned themselves during the Vietnam war. Americans little understood this because of the differences in religious backgrounds.

During the first few centuries of the Christian church, the subject of suicide was far from fixed. The Bible did not specifically condemn the act, though some passages possibly inferred it. Nevertheless, there are records of Jews killing themselves en masse rather than being captured, such as at Masada.

The first four centuries were particularly tough for Christians. During this time, many committed suicide. Their religion was generally illegal; they often lost their jobs; they were murdered for sport in coliseums. In fact, some observers felt becoming a Christian was equal to committing suicide. The persecutions all but guaranteed the convert's death in one form or another.

Life became so difficult for Christians and the promises of heaven so appealing that many became voluntary martyrs. By doing this, they reasoned, they could gain immediate access to heaven and a martyr's crown. The church would take the responsibility of supporting the family, and they no longer had to fight the continuous struggle with sin. This practice may not have been as bizarre as it seems. Periods of hardship always increase the number of suicides, as evidenced by the Depression and by Jews under Nazism. Some of the oppressions faced by the early Christians will match any in history.

Suicide was also looked upon with favor among those who were protecting their virginity. Many cultures, including some Christian, have considered self-destruction as the preferable alternative.

In the fifth century, one man's writing probably did more than anything else to halt the tolerance toward suicide. The man was Augustine and the book was *The City of God*. He equated suicide with murder, referring to it as the worst of sins. This attitude served as the basis for our civil and ecclesiastical laws for fifteen hundred years. The courts eventually labeled the attempt as a felony and distributed heavy prison terms.

Official church councils prohibited funeral rites

25

for suicides even though common criminals had the right to the ceremony. Later, suicides were refused burial in church cemeteries (1284, Synod of Nimes). When the church was in power, it often attacked problems by edict rather than compassion.

As some courts became uncomfortable with this approach, they attempted to remove the moral implications and declare the person insane. Now the suicide victim had both his soul and mind condemned, while his body had already perished.

Governments tried to make suicide such a horrible affair that no one would dare try it. It is questionable if they successfully dissuaded anyone, but they certainly made it difficult for the survivors. Regularly the government confiscated the victim's land, leaving the family destitute. British law demanded such a victim be buried at a crossroads and a stake driven through his heart to pin his ghost down. The same sentiment was transferred to North America. In 1660, the state of Massachusetts buried its victims on a common highway and dumped a cartload of stones on the grave.

In the Renaissance of the fourteenth and fifteenth centuries, free thinkers broke from church tradition and began to paint suicide in a more tolerable light. They saw theological problems as irrelevant. Ending one's life was purely a personal prerogative, they said.

Eighteenth-century philosophers went a step further and discussed the merits of suicide. Joann Robeck (b. 1672) added up the relative benefits of life and decided death was far preferable. Jean-

Jacques Rousseau was impressed with the defense of self-destruction. David Hume saw mental problems but no moral issue.

Who is right? Which of these Christians and non-Christians have been closest to the mind of God? Where ought we to stand along the continuum that stretches from total condemnation to unquestioning endorsement?

THREE

FROM GOD'S PERSPECTIVE

MOST CHRISTIANS FIND IT IMPOSSIBLE to straighten out their feelings about suicide without discussing how God fits into the picture. Historically, and even recently, we have been told by some that God will reject the suicide victim.

One Sunday school teacher told his class of young people, "Well, I imagine that the person who commits suicide is so far from Christ that he would be lost." The instructor was doubtless doing his best. But his answer reflects a misunderstanding of both the individual and God. This thought pattern tends to depict the victim as a moral fiend who has crossed the border into the eerie and hideous.

The fact is, many victims hold on to their faith

after they have lost everything else. They find the pressures of life impossible to cope with. Some see the next life as the only hope left. In a euphoric state they imagine themselves being translated into the presence of God. Their faith is so strong, they can hardly wait to enter a land where there is no pain or tears. They may feel they have held onto the ledge by their fingertips for years. Now they want to let go and fall peacefully into a land of tranquillity.

From the earliest days of Christianity, believers have found death preferable to the cruelties of life. Even the apostle Paul inwardly weighed his yearning to die: "For to me, to live is Christ and to die is gain. If I am to go on living in the body, this will mean fruitful labor for me. Yet, what shall I choose? I do not know! I am torn between the two: I desire to depart and be with Christ, which is better by far" (Phil. 1: 21-23).

Paul, of course, should not be described as suicidal on the basis of these verses, but he does consider death a friend. If forced to choose between the benefits of life and the assets of death, he saw little contest.

A lady in her eighties who lived in Kansas is a good example of the principle. The doctors diagnosed her case as cancer of the throat. Bravely, she submitted herself to cobalt treatments that made her terribly ill.

At first, her attitude was determined and fixed. She considered it wrong to ask God to take her life. Her confidence in God's timing was unshakable. As the pain increased and she became totally dependent on drugs, however, she finally asked God to take her home. Her desire for the joys of death became enormous.

The Christian's faith has done an excellent job of teaching the good features of heaven. In the process, many Christians have hurried their journey across the river.

In modern times a famous couple, Henry and Elizabeth Van Dusen, chose to vacate in favor of eternity. Dr. Van Dusen was a theological professor and very active in the Euthanasia Society, which promotes "voluntary euthanasia." Aged and failing in health, the couple decided to call a halt, and each took his own life. Whatever the merits or defects of their action, they viewed it not as an act of faithless paganism but rather as a demonstration of their Christian belief.

But what of the person who has cursed God either verbally or in writing before he killed himself? Surely this one has gone too far and has entered the pale of the hopeless.

As we have mentioned previously, the person who commits the desperate suicide is usually someone who has lost his judgment. He may write a note filled with vile contempt for his wife when, in fact, she was his great love. He may denounce God and Christ in his frustration and at the same time long to go into their presence.

Is there some way to fathom the mind of God in all of this heartache, pain and confusion? Probably the only source that will help us is the Bible. While nature gives us some clues to God, it gives us nothing concerning our present discussion. If the Bible does not speak to the issue, then we are left to our own deductions.

We must say the Bible does not directly teach anything on the subject of suicide. The word doesn't appear, nor is the theme dealt with. Some people begin with the sixth commandment, then define suicide as self-murder, and say therefore that it is condemned by God. Augustine felt this way. Thomas Aquinas went further. He labeled suicide as the most fatal of all sins because the victim could not repent of it. But since we cannot find scriptures that specifically condemn suicide, we must take a secondary and less dependable route. We must look for examples and principles that might apply.

Examples of suicide are scarce in the Bible, and practically no time is spent discussing the ethical consideration. These examples can be studied at the reader's convenience: Saul and his armor-bearer (1 Sam. 31:4-5); Ahithophel (2 Sam. 17:23); Zimri (1 Kings 16:18-19); and Judas (Matt. 27:5; Acts 1:18).

Technically, the death of Samson can also be described as a suicide. After his entrapment, blinding, and imprisonment, Samson had one last request. He asked God to let him pull down the pillars of the pagan temple and kill his enemies, the Philistines. He also asked, "Let me die with the Philistines." God appears to have answered his prayer (Judg. 16:23-31).

It may be that we can draw few practical conclusions from these illustrations; nevertheless, this is all the direct material available.

FACING THE TRAGEDY

But if we turn to study the nature and temperament of God, we can make several observations.

1. Jesus Christ was highly tolerant toward people who had personal problems. There were times when he denounced, scathed, and became angry at people (Mark 3:5); however, these were for the self-righteous who thought they had no needs. Jesus extended arms of love toward parents with sick children, those who had diseases, and those who were alone and misunderstood.

He put it most succinctly when he said, "It is not the healthy who need a doctor, but the sick" (Luke 5:31). We would find it difficult to picture Christ short-tempered and unloving toward someone who was so pressed and confused that he had trouble thinking correctly.

2. Jesus displayed a forgiving attitude toward the suffering. There is nothing unforgivable about suicide. Christ taught us that "every sin and blasphemy will be forgiven men" (Matt. 12:31).

As we mentioned earlier, Aquinas objected to the possibility of forgiving the suicide victim since the deceased could no longer ask for cleansing. But God forgives us even when we don't ask for it. One case in point is the story of the paralytic who was lowered through the roof by his four friends. "When Jesus saw their faith, he said to the paralytic, 'Son, your sins are forgiven'" (Mark 2:5).

The story does not say the sick man asked for forgiveness, and yet Jesus offered it freely. When we make up rules that are prerequisites to God's forgiveness, we walk up wobbly stairs.

3. Jesus Christ offered acceptance to the heavily burdened. Christ was not in the habit of adding crushing loads to those who were already encumbered. He didn't throw millstones at struggling swimmers, nor did he lock the gates to a staggering traveler.

Jesus summed up his attitude toward the overwhelmed by saying, "Come to me, all you who are weary and burdened, and I will give you rest. Take my yoke upon you and learn from me, for I am gentle and humble in heart, and you will find rest for your souls. For my yoke is easy and my burden is light" (Matt. 11:28-30).

Before one can decide God's outlook on suicide, he must first decide the condition of the victim. Is he a mean murderer who turned to suicide because he was a plotting fiend? Or was he a confused person whose heart hurt and who found it no longer possible to carry his internal and external problems? Did he hold those cares until finally his knees buckled and he fell to the ground? If we see the suicide victim as the latter, we will have no trouble understanding how God feels toward him.

Another important question is how we feel about God. Every tragedy in life is a rattling experience. After a loved one commits suicide, many Christians are shaken in their faith. Where was God when this horror happened? Why didn't he stop it?

It would not be unheard of for a Christian to be angry at God. Even though he may fight to squelch or muffle his emotions, inside he would like to scream out, "How could you let this happen?" If we don't work out our feelings, the results may be disastrous. Trying to smother anger may only cause smoldering inside. That can make someone ashamed of how he really feels about God and refuse to admit his questions.

Others will externalize their hostility. They may dump their faith in God, thinking he is a heartless despot. Bitterness will become their permanent jacket.

We need to be reminded that God does not control everything in our lives; he does not make decisions for us. Sometimes we want to believe he does, because it sounds idyllic. God is compassionate and caring, but he chooses not to control our actions. God is not responsible for everything we ever do; he allows us to make many of our own choices.

Christ pointed directly to our free will when he said, "How often I have longed to gather your children together, as a hen gathers her chicks under her wings, but you were not willing" (Matt. 23:37).

God's heart must ache at the sight of war, crime, rape, child abuse, and suicide. Someday he promises to give us a better world without crying and pain. But he does not protect us from every tragedy. The faithful believer will have his heart broken many times in a twisted world. But Christ promises us warm care while we wait to meet him face to face.

Paul put it this way, "Neither height nor depth, nor anything else in all creation, will be able to separate us from the love of God that is in Christ Jesus our Lord" (Rom. 8:39).

FOUR

WAS IT
MY FAULT?

PEOPLE DO NOT USUALLY die without hurting everyone close to them. We each are encircled by eight to ten relatives and special friends. With a suicide, the pain is particularly acute for those left behind; the tragic event will cut them deeply, and most will never get completely over it.

A survivor's first feelings are probably a mixture of disbelief and shame: This horror could not really have happened; but it has. Eventually these initial reactions may sink into hostility and guilt.

Hostility is hard to handle. If the survivors are not careful, they may hate the deceased the rest of their lives, programming themselves for a bitter, distorted future. Hopefully, Christians will find some way to forgive.

FACING THE TRAGEDY

As our feelings turn inward, we will have to handle the ultimate personal question: Was this terrible death really my fault?

A family on the West Coast decided to move to another city. Their teenage girl, Karen, was shocked at first, but then said nothing. Her personality began to change, and she grew increasingly silent. One morning they found her dead, hanging in the basement.

Are her parents to blame for Karen's death? Or was she facing other problems, and moving presented a final blow? If so, this final straw could have come from any number of sources. Failure in a class or being dropped by a boyfriend could have proved equally fatal. Most suicides are not by impulse; rather, a person who commits suicide is usually overloaded with internal problems. Eventually some event may tip the load, and he will kill himself. The final weight could come from a number of directions, and the person supplying the ultimate reason could be entirely innocent.

This is not to say the survivors do not share a certain amount of guilt, but it is important not to lose perspective. Each of us could be kinder if we chose to. All of us can remember times when we were inconsiderate to a parent, brother, or wife. Guilt is a common denominator no matter what the cause of death. Whenever a death occurs, we rehearse our failures: Why didn't we take her out the night she wanted to go? We really could have bought the coat. We should have volunteered to do the dishes when she was so tired.

It would be unrealistic to say, "Cheer up, you did everything you could." Who has done everything he could? None of us. In the aftermath of death, it is fruitless to pretend we did each thing correctly. We only resent the person who unknowingly tries to reassure us that our behavior was perfect.

But admitting our mistakes is a far cry from saying we caused a suicide. Except for a few oddities in life, people do not normally cause others to kill themselves. To insist we did everything correctly is to stifle reality. To assume the total blame is to carry an unreasonable and unfair burden. To accept our imperfection is the beginning of a healing process.

Those who are Christians can use a normal cleansing process. Admit the mistakes and give them to God (1 John 1: 9); he will forgive and cleanse us. There is no need to bottle up the sin and guilt and carry them around the rest of our lives. God promises to heal our guilt, and he sincerely hopes we will accept his healing.

Many people will turn down this cleansing because they want to punish themselves. They are determined to suffer, and only a daily flogging will make them content. This type of defacing is a form of self-pity. They feel sorry for themselves and gain satisfaction from suffering. This method of abuse can only hurt everyone involved.

The person who tortures himself could wreck his own body and personality. In the process, he will also hurt those who are close to him: children, family, friends, coworkers. He cannot possibly help the deceased by prolonged grief. To refuse forgiveness can be a destructive act that serves no good purpose.

When guilt is not handled properly, the results are often disastrous. Some survivors go on to kill themselves as a sort of atonement for what they believe they did. Others refuse to marry again. They believe they drove the first husband to his death, and they are certain they affect people adversely.

A common tragedy is the reluctance to love, to give heart and emotions to another person; they are afraid they will be crushed again. Some children find it difficult to trust anyone after a parent's suicide.

Those who survive must be determined to live. As much as possible, they need to rebuild their lives and accept the healing that comes by forgiveness. In some cases, friends and relatives can be cruel. They may say things that are cutting and hard to forget. But we need to remember they, too, face an unreasonable pressure.

Jolene's in-laws fell into this category. When their son, Ed, killed himself, they lashed out in all directions. They tried to find someone to blame. Their son would not have done this unless he was driven to it. They decided it was Jolene's fault. Overcome with anger, they told her exactly how they felt.

How did this accusation help anyone? Jolene loved Ed intensely. The charges only added to her grief. Ed's parents redirected their hostility but did nothing to remove it.

We each experience enough real guilt without added pain from exploding accusations.

A minister visited a family the day after the husband had shot himself. He was not pushy but wanted to help if he could.

The wife was belligerent. She did not want to talk about the death. "It was the only smart thing the slob ever did for us," she said. She did not attend the funeral. But did she really despise her husband? Not necessarily. It would be hard to measure her contribution to the suicide. Possibly she is innocent and merely crying out from the pain.

Natural death and accidents have their particular weight. But suicide has its special pain. When someone says, "He killed himself" or "He died by his own hand," we are stunned. We ask, "Why would he choose to end his life and leave? Why would a person want to do that?" And our answers are not always rational.

The surviving family feels rejected. The victim has said, in effect, he does not want to live with them. They feel their love was not enough to keep him going. The survivors, however, only see half the story. In this case, they only see their part. The victim may have been thinking the exact opposite.

When Earl attempted suicide, he felt differently than many expect. He had two wonderful children and a wife whom he adored. But his feelings of inadequacy were becoming overbearing. As he became increasingly confused, his logic followed this pattern. He loved his family intensely. Because of his supposed inabilities, Earl felt he could not hold on to his job. He considered himself strange and possibly insane.

FACING THE TRAGEDY

In his thinking, he saw himself as harmful to the people he loved. There was nothing he enjoyed more than wrestling with his children on the floor or holding his wife. But he was sure in the long run he was only hurting them. He decided to end it.

We protest! Earl was wrong. That is beside the point. It is the way he thought. He tried to end his life while feeling love and despair simultaneously.

Earl's loss of judgment kept him from seeing the facts. He could not realize that by committing suicide, he would do his family far more harm than he could do them in life. If he had completed the act, his young children may have felt totally rejected. But Earl could not sort his feelings out.

Parents, spouses, and children will suffer the most. Yet in many cases this pain is the last thing the victim intended.

The amount of confusion faced by the victim can often be seen in the notes left behind. Some are mixed with hate and love. Even the author may not be able to explain the strange structure. The victim may try to provoke his reader into hating him. In his shifting, almost romantic logic he may think his wife will be better off if she hates him. Consequently, he says he hates her. This reasoning makes sense to him.

One of the more famous suicide notes reads simply, "Dear Mary, I hate you. Love, John." What does this message say? The note indicates the author's tremendous stress and ambivalence. He hurts deeply.

The victim often has a way of rationalizing an

idyllic future for those he leaves behind. He fantasizes his wife remarried to a handsome hero. The children are playing happily in the backyard of a stylish home. The wife is barbecuing with a broad smile across her face. It doesn't occur to him that the real picture will be the extreme opposite. The family may end up on welfare, and the children will wrestle with deep psychological scars.

Some sad notes wish only the best for someone they warmly love. "I'm tired. There must be something fine for you. Love, Bill."

It would be naive to think every suicide victim was filled with gentle love. A note or final phone call can be packed with the cruelist venom. The victim is hostile. He feels he has been treated terribly, and he spells out just who has done it. Certainly some of these tirades are serious; sometimes they are even accurate.

Most victims, however, are confused rather than lucid. She may see herself lying on the floor unconscious with an empty pill bottle beside her head. Her husband or boyfriend walks into the room. Shocked, he kneels and gathers her into his arms.

She thoroughly enjoys the scene. In reality, this is exactly what she has wanted. In her confusion she is unable to fathom the grief she is causing. She sees only her personal needs and imagines death to be a moment of tenderness.

Suicide is a confusing death. People who often want to live are killing themselves. Those who desperately want love are cutting it off. Those who may have had little to do with the tragedy are left to suffer and sort out the guilt. Suicide has so little to recommend it.

Those who must deal with the aftermath do well to begin immediately. The longer the facts are avoided or denied, the more difficult the recovery could be.

Years ago, I was asked to conduct a funeral for a retiree who had shot himself. He had no hobbies, and the age of sixty-five always frightened him. Within a week after he got his gold watch, he turned a rifle on himself.

The family was stricken and compassionate, but they were also candid from the beginning. We talked about the suicide and used the word. During the funeral we made a couple of references to it.

His children and grandchildren, his wife and sisters were going to have enough troubles. They decided not to complicate things by trying to deny the facts.

Journalist James Wechsler has written a moving account of the suicide of his son Michael. From the beginning, he was surprised at everyone's desire to hide the facts. The police were more than willing to alter the evidence so no one would know. They wanted to protect the family's good name and position.

A clear conscience can be obtained by facing reality, not by running. The survivors need to recognize they did some things they would like to change, but they did not do everything wrong. Coping with the truth is the surest road to healing.

FIVE

IS SUICIDE INSANITY?

"PEOPLE WHO KILL THEMSELVES must be nuts!"

That is a frequent reaction. We are sure something must have snapped in a person's mind or that part of his brain has decayed. It is an important issue, one that has to be solved before we can be helpful.

Insanity is difficult to define. Experts disagree on who is actually "crazy." Some authorities even believe everything is a learned or adopted behavior, and insanity does not exist.

The United Press International reported the story of a youth who tried to kill herself in Hartford, Connecticut. She slashed her wrists and arms and then ran to the steps of a church. As she held a razor to her throat, a crowd of 300 gathered to watch.

The spectators began cheering and screaming, "Do your thing, sister!" Someone threw a bottle and hit the tense teenager. Each time she motioned as if to cut herself, the crowd sent up a cheer. When she collapsed from loss of blood, the audience applauded. Who was insane, the girl or the crowd?

In order to get a handle on the subject, we will equate insanity with psychotic behavior. This means that a person drifts in and out of reality. One minute he is mowing his lawn; the next minute he thinks he is the king of Spain. He may withdraw to his room and stay there for a week. There may be moments of severe illusion and hallucination.

Ron is a typical example of a psychotic suicide. He is in his late thirties and has been suicidal on and off for sixteen years. Most of this time he has been in and out of hospitals. Periodically he hears voices telling him what to do. At times he has had unbearable pain in his head.

Ron experiences periods of extreme violence. He has broken two ribs of a hospital orderly, destroyed furniture, and frequently he has had to be restrained. When the voices and pain subside, Ron is released. He has not held a job more than a couple of months. Eventually he always ends up under medical care.

It is hard to say why he acts the way he does. Is it a conscious choice on his part, or is something uncontrollable happening? Whatever the cause, Ron is psychotic and suicidal. But he is the exception.

Many authorities believe only 4 percent of suicides are psychotic. The person who killed himself may have gone to work yesterday and put in a fairly good shift.

Many casual friends will remark after a suicide, "He seemed all right to me. He was quiet, but I never would have guessed." The reason he seemed normal was because he *was* fairly normal. The victim did not chew wallpaper. He was hurting but not insane.

The following categories of non insane suicide help us understand why people attempt to kill themselves.

The *impulse* suicide is someone who acts quickly in rage. The girl is told she could not go to the dance. She races to her room and swallows twenty sleeping pills. She believes she has adequate reason to end her life. This type of attempt is not as frequent as we might think.

A *hopeless* suicide is someone who sees no point to life. He is often depressed; nothing seems to go the way he wants it. He feels there is no solution. Why live out a life of misery? One movie star left a suicide note that simply read, "I'm bored." It's a "what's the use" death.

The *illness* suicide results from people being unable to cope with their physical problems. The father of a high-ranking member of the Carter administration made this decision. He had watched two of his close relatives die from inoperable cancer. When the doctors gave him the same diagnosis, he selected a pistol instead.

Lack of communication is another rationale often used. The person feels no one is listening, no one cares, no one can possibly understand how much he hurts. Frustrated, he turns to something drastic. The person may be completely mistaken. There may be plenty of people who want to listen, many who genuinely feel for him. But since he feels no one can appreciate his dilemma, he decides to act. He wants his acquaintances to "see what I have done so they will know how badly I hurt." Then, supposedly, they will sympathize and try to help.

A *noble* suicide is a more ancient desire to die for dignity. Women used to kill themselves to avoid rape. Generals would commit suicide if their army were defeated. The early Christians chose to die at their own hand rather than be slain by gladiators or torn apart by lions.

Some suicides do not fit into any of these categories. But most suicides have some rationale to them, even though the thinking may be faulty and totally unacceptable to the majority of mankind. It may be totally unacceptable to God. But in most cases, there is some vague attempt to think the problem through.

Most suicides are not raving maniacs. They have lost or distorted their sense of judgment, but they are not insane.

Historians tell us General Custer most likely saved his last bullet at Little Big Horn. When the outcome was no longer in doubt, he reportedly turned his pistol on himself. There may have been a strong logic to what he did.

The influence of drugs often pushes the individual across the threshold from rational to psychotic behavior. Imagine an individual who has difficulty coping with his mounting problems. The pressures are affecting his judgment process. In his vacillating condition, he decides to turn to drugs. The drug abuse helps him escape. That's what he wanted. But instead of making him better able to face reality, it diminishes his faculties. Now his mind does go adrift. He may start to swing in and out of reality. In the final analysis, drugs may cause him to come closer to suicide. The inability to think clearly can only hurt his chances of survival.

When Christians discuss effects on the human mind, we must consider the role Satan plays. There is no doubt he is concerned with the disasters that confront man, and there is also no doubt he influences us as much as he can, but we must not give him too much credit. Our natural instincts are to blame everything on someone else. We are in love because of Cupid. We have been unfaithful to our wife because of Satan. We are a financial failure because of unscrupulous competitors. That approach is too simplistic.

Two things we can say with certainty on the subject. One, God holds us responsible for our own decisions and actions. Two, Satan cannot affect our lives if we do not let him.

Man is capable of doing good and evil by himself, and so the Bible gives us much practical instruction. God made us moral characters who, when given the proper information, have the ability to act on it.

FACING THE TRAGEDY

The Bible is also definite on the limitations of Satan. "Submit yourselves, then, to God. Resist the devil, and he will flee from you" (James 4:7). Satan cannot do anything to us unless we willingly give him the opportunity. It is a cop-out to blame tragedy on the devil. As long as we accept the responsibility for our own decisions, there is hope.

Despite the potential victim's confusion, many of his actions are deliberate. He can calculate and reason rather well.

Many have visited a doctor, counselor, or other form of professional before making the attempt. They have dropped clues or given hints of drastic despair. Frequently there is evidence of searching for help but of not being able to accept it. It is as if a gigantic wall stands between them and assistance. They approach the wall but see no possible way to climb it.

Some readers may want to protest. They will insist that anyone who attempts to end his own life is mentally ill; otherwise, he would never do it. And there are capable authorities who agree with this position. It really becomes a question of degrees and definitions. The person who tries to end his life is mentally troubled. That's a fair and dependable observation. But labeling it "insane" or "crazy" may not be warranted by the facts.

Probably the most common mental trouble among suicides is depression, and it occurs most among those over forty. Without a doubt, if a person has developed an aura of hopelessness, he has to become depressed. It is, if you will, a normal abnormality. The general population also suffers from a high frequency of depression.

The issue of sanity and insanity becomes important for the people involved. Suppose a nineteen-year-old college student in a siege of despair tries to take his life. After the troubles have subsided, he then tries to rebuild his future. The shadow hanging over his shoulder is the thought that he is really crazy. He becomes haunted at the prospect of being "nuts."

He needs to be reassured that, despite his dark hour, he is not insane. All the potential of tomorrow is his. Counseling could help him erase a few cobwebs or get a couple cars back on the track. But there is a world of difference between needing some help and being crazy.

Dr. Paul Barkman, formerly of Fuller Seminary and now in private practice, points out a needed axiom. People are not as calmly rational as we would like to believe. We do not place everything into neat pigeonholes. We hurt the people we love. We enjoy food until it is harmful. Is it then strange that we try to solve our problems by killing ourselves?

A hundred years ago men were executed in England for trying to commit suicide. Can the men who fashioned that law be labeled as sane?

If the inability to think straight equals insanity, we are a desperate lot.

SIX

WE HAVE A LOT
IN COMMON

IT WAS ONE OF THE MOST UNUSUAL phone calls I ever received. A local funeral director wanted me to take a service for a twenty-one-year-old suicide victim.

"The parents did not want any service, but we talked them into it," he said. "They will agree if you can keep it to seven minutes."

I went with mixed emotions. Sure, I wanted to help, but I wondered if it were possible.

The father was a highly successful executive, born in Germany. His only son had a crippling disease that was paralyzing both of his hands. At the time of his death, he could only use one finger on his right hand. He had graduated from a technical school and had an excellent mind. He had looked forward to the prospect of following his father's career, but when the disease struck, the future seemed dismal. He thought he had better act while he still could. Parked on a lonely road, he turned a pistol on himself.

Both father and mother were furious. They had struggled for years to help their son. They had kept their courage despite the overwhelming odds in his physical condition. How could he treat them so badly as to kill himself? His parents did not even want to see his body.

It is easy to feel contempt for people who commit suicide. We act as if they were inferior, feeling "That coward bailed out, while I stayed to fight."

What we have forgotten is how much we are really like them. Maybe the reason we become so angry is because we realize how threatening the subject is. All of us are vulnerable. We have learned to hate the kinks in our own lives; therefore, we hate them when we see them glaring in someone else.

Authorities estimate over 90 percent of us at some time think about our own suicide. Maybe it's only a passing thought. Sometimes we wonder if death is not a better alternative than some of the things we face in life. However innocent the contemplation, most of us have entertained the possibility.

People naturally balk when the 90 percent figure is used. We find it hard to believe that many individuals consider suicide sometime in their lives. Nevertheless, most studies indicate this to be the case.

FACING THE TRAGEDY

Recently a psychologist took a sample at a large university. He asked 165 students if they had ever thought of killing themselves. Of those, 132 said they had. In order to reach the 90 percent statistic, seventeen more must consider it. They have the rest of their lives before them. No doubt the percentage will hold up.

A young woman said, "Sure I've thought about it. When I first got my divorce, I saw no way I could raise three small children. Welfare could not do the job, and my ex was no help."

This mother cannot be described as chronically suicidal. But she faced some circumstances that caused her to think about it.

Another group goes the second step. They begin to act out the particulars in their minds. What will they use? Where might they do it? It is no longer a passing fantasy. They wonder about the mechanics.

A third group are those who gather materials. They check to see how many pills are in the cupboard. Possibly they stop by the bridge, wondering if there is a guard rail.

Most of us fit into one of these categories. Maybe not for long, but we have visited these thoughts. Having these feelings does not make us worthless or unstable. It merely indicates our brotherhood in humanity. My problems aren't so different from yours except in intensity.

The Bible understands this identity better than most individuals. Paul presented this axiom: "No temptation has seized you except what is common to man. And God is faithful; he will not let you be tempted beyond what you can bear. But when you are tempted, he will also provide a way out so that you can stand up under it" (1 Cor. 10:13).

The verse is a message of hope. It is also a reaffirmation of our commonness. Suicide is a natural temptation that normal people weigh.

Jesus was concerned because the Pharisees detested prostitutes. They were not worried about helping them; rather, they believed they did the work of God by condemning their fellow humans. Christ saw the process differently. He considered prostitution wrong, so he tried to help the prostitutes. Likewise, we would do better to consider suicide wrong and try to help the potential victim.

One day I heard a syndicated radio commentator taking scathing swipes at those who committed suicide. They were cowards to him. The courageous people were the ones who fought and lived.

Why was he pressing this tirade? Did he think he would save some lives by berating them? Did he really believe they were cowards? Or was suicide such a personal threat that he could only handle it in anger? Whatever he accomplished, the gentleman failed to show any understanding or compassion.

If we think we are better than the would-be suicide, we disqualify ourselves. We may be different, but definitely no better.

To appreciate how common the experience is, we should consider how many try it. Statistics are shaky. Not everyone who attempts suicide registers at the local courthouse. There could be half a million tries in the United States annually. Writers in the field, including Choron and Stengel, believe there are at least ten attempts for every completion. Shneidman puts the figure at eight to one.

People who attempt suicide, and their families, suffer a great deal from the haunting effects. If each person has eight close relatives or friends, that means four million people are affected annually. Over a ten-year period, it is plausible that forty million Americans have been affected by someone's attempt at suicide.

We are a large and bothered fraternity. Contempt for the victim only adds to our troubles. If we can accept the suicide victim as a person like us, we will find it much easier to forgive him. This is an essential step to our own recovery.

A Californian described the continuing anguish of her family. "Fifteen years ago my brother attempted suicide," she said. "He swallowed a bottle of pills but somehow pulled through. It doesn't bother me particularly, but my mother will never get over it. She can't forgive him for doing this to us."

Some authorities believe we seldom forgive a suicide; Dr. Shneidman believes it is never totally forgiven. We feel the person has betrayed us or rejected those around him. How could he bail out? Why did he turn down our love? What is wrong with me that he couldn't stand to stay here? His action is a personal insult. The emphasis is "me," and we soon forget the hurt the victim faced.

It takes a great deal of love and grace to forgive the person. It is only human to nurse a deep, painful wound. But part of the Christian hope is to rise above and love when otherwise it would be all but impossible.

A middle-aged man found his wife's body soon after she shot herself. She had threatened to take her life several times. Now the man was crushed with grief and confusion. Fortunately, he had a close relationship with another Christian, in this case, his pastor. The minister spent many hours encouraging the man to talk about it. They fielded questions back and forth. Each admitted it when he had no answers. The pastor often read relevant Scriptures to him, and they prayed together.

Finally, the husband came to see his wife as the victim and not himself. He could see her hurt more than his own. The day eventually came when he forgave his wife for killing herself, but first he had to stop nursing his own wound.

It is easy to understand why most survivors never forgive. There is no simple way to do it. It is also easy to see why some Christians can forgive—because there is something special in Jesus Christ. "Be kind and compassionate to one another, forgiving each other, just as in Christ God forgave you" (Eph. 4:32).

A mother in Nebraska was left with three small children. Her husband could not cope with the pressures of life and so killed himself. The family sank immediately into poverty. For all of their growing years, the children struggled for food and clothing. It is no wonder they were never able to forgive him; they paid painfully for his act.

But in reality, they chose to pay double when it wasn't necessary. They had to pay the price of his absence; they were stuck with that bill. But each member also paid the price of nonforgiveness. They carried around the pain of holding a grudge against a person long gone.

How a person could take his own life and leave his family in turmoil is difficult to understand and certainly impossible to justify. The only hope that remains is the ability to forgive.

Jesus Christ is extremely understanding. He knows there are some situations in which forgiveness is almost impossible. Husbands usually find it difficult to forgive the unfaithful act of a wife, and vice versa. But Christ wishes they could.

It is hard to forgive a suicide victim. It's even difficult to forgive someone who attempts it. Christ doesn't condemn us when we can't. But for our sake, he really wishes we would.

PART TWO

FACTS ABOUT SUICIDE

SEVEN

A LOOK AT
THE FACTS

WHAT WE BELIEVED thirty years ago about suicide
may have to be reevaluated today as we have access
to more facts.

Statistics on suicide are improving, although they
are still sparse. Possibly half the incidents are not
reported correctly. In some cases, the suicide is covered up. In other cases, we can't be sure whether the
death was a suicide or not. At other times, the victim
takes extensive pains to disguise the real cause. Consequently, new facts are coming to light but only in a
piecemeal fashion.

The facts remain fluid because regrettably,
suicide is subject to fads. During a particular decade, pressures on a segment of society may sharply

increase self-inflicted deaths. One of the peak years in the United States was 1932. The number of suicides reached record highs. The year 1977 showed another drastic increase.

The following is a brief summary of the facts and trends as they presently stand. Many of these are discussed at length in other parts of the book.

● *Fact:* Most people do *not* leave a suicide note.

Contrary to popular belief, most suicides (about 85 percent) have not written out a reason for their act. This may be because they have difficulty expressing their real feelings; we know a high percentage of suicide attempts complain of an inability to communicate. Many suicide notes that are left are too confusing to be helpful.

This makes the job of suicide study all the more difficult. In some large population areas, the coroner will not list a death as suicide unless there is a note. Thus, perhaps only fifteen percent of the suicides are recorded as such.

● *Fact:* Most suicides occur during the daytime.

The hours of 3:00 to 6:00 P.M. are the peak time. Even though a person may be suffering from a night or more of sleeplessness, the actual act frequently takes place in the day.

● *Fact:* Suicide affects all segments of society.

People of all ages, races, and economics are choosing this way out of life. There had been a feeling that suicide was more for the well-to-do, a luxury the workingman and poor could not afford, but latest findings reveal a democratic flavor.

However, some groups do seem to stand out.

Suicide among American Indians is six times the national average. Indians sixteen to twenty-four, single, and with parental instability are a high risk. The problems of poverty, unemployment, isolation, and cultural conflict prove too much. The suicide rate among blacks is also higher than previously thought. The lack of a father image may play a significant role. For those under thirty-five, the percentage of black suicides is greater than for whites.

• *Fact:* There is a sharp increase in female suicides.

The old statistics indicated more women attempted suicide but more men completed it. Though this is still true, the trend is in the other direction. Now women are turning to more violent means. It is no longer safe to think of a lady lying across a bed with an empty pill bottle, hoping to be found; Women are turning to guns.

Experts suspect the changing role of women is causing this increase. Many women are bewildered about their identity: are they businesswomen, or housewives, or both? Some are finding it too difficult to cope.

• *Fact:* Suicides in the 16-24 age group is the fastest-growing category.

In the past twenty years this group has tripled its number of suicides. One half of these are involved in drug abuse of some nature.

• *Fact:* Most suicidal persons want to live.

The key word here is *ambivalent.* They want to die, but they want to stay. They have come to the end of

61

their rope, but they wish there were more to life. Consequently, many attempters will place themselves in a setting in which they could easily be found. They may deny this to themselves, but they still arrange the circumstances to leave options.

- *Fact:* Most suicidal people are not crazy.

They may have lost their best judgment, but few are psychotic. Most don't imagine themselves to be Napoleon or see devils chasing them.

- *Fact:* Suicide is *not* hereditary.

Suicide is not an organic problem passed from parent to child. Suicide does, however, place serious pressure on the family. Children often need help in facing this crushing tragedy.

- *Fact:* Christians commit suicide.

Definitely. Statistics obviously are not available, but plenty of examples are. One pastor said, "I had funerals for two active members this past month. They both committed suicide."

The secretary of a large, conservative church in the Midwest took her own life. As shattering as it is, the facts seem irrefutable. Hopefully the ratio of suicide victims is less among Christians than among the general population.

- *Fact:* Children commit suicide.

Every day in the United States, approximately two children ages 9-15 intentionally end their own lives.

- *Fact:* People thinking about suicide seek help.

The common saying has always been, "If he talks about suicide, don't worry." The feeling today is the opposite. Most people (eight out of ten) who attempt suicide first try to discuss it with someone. If a person suggests suicide, he should be taken seriously. Whatever his intentions, he has definitely lit a red light. He is hurting and wants someone to listen.

• *Fact:* Professional people are high risks.

Doctors, dentists, and lawyers kill themselves at a rate of five to seven times that of the general population. Many of them have no one to talk to. The emotional strain caused by their professional responsibilities is often enormous. Some are too proud to share their problems. Psychiatrists lead the list in self-destruction. But suicides among the unskilled, minorities, and youth are on the increase. Some experts note that artists and farmers have particularly low suicide rates.

• *Fact:* Guns are a large factor.

Almost half of the completed suicides involve a gun. The person who selects a gun has reached a final desperation. He probably has no illusions of half-dying. After guns, the most popular means are pills, drugs, and hanging. Further study could demonstrate vehicular suicide as the number one means in the United States.

• *Fact:* Suicide prevention centers are widely used.

The first one was started in 1906 by Baptist minister Harry Warren. By 1958 the concept had spread rapidly. Today there are over two hundred centers nationwide. Trained personnel are on hand twenty-four hours a day to answer phone calls. Tens of thousands are helped monthly to overcome a crisis.

FACTS ABOUT SUICIDE

- *Fact:* Certain months are peak seasons.

April and May see the most suicides. The concepts of spring, love, and success are often too much to handle. The news of other people enjoying themselves is often hard for the depressed person to take. December is a low month generally, but Christmas itself brings a flurry.

Friday, Monday, and Sunday are the most frequent days.

- *Fact:* Suicide attempts are a national epidemic.

There are no accurate figures on attempts at suicide—many are not reported to the police or doctors. But those who work in the field give astronomical estimates. Some authorities believe two-to-four hundred thousand people attempt suicide each year. Other experts take the number well over one million. Whichever is accurate, the problem is acute.

Perhaps one reason for the sudden rise may be a simple case of better records. Many suicides in the past have been listed under other categories. In the near future, a sudden increase in statistics can be expected because of improved record keeping.

- *Fact:* Alcoholism is a form of suicide.

Those with experience in the field feel the two problems are often similar. The victim has trouble coping with his problems. He looks for a way to escape. His feelings are mixed, and he wants to get out—but just for a while.

Alcoholism can be a slow form of death. The victim looks at himself in much the same way as the suicide.

• *Fact:* Many individuals can be talked out of suicide.

Among psychologists there is a difference of opinion. There is some truth to the statement, "If a person really wants to kill himself, no one can stop him." It is also true, however, that most potential suicides do not want to die.

In many cases, the feeling of despair is temporary. A certain crisis or disappointment may have triggered the desire to end it all. If this storm can be weathered, the individual may never resort to suicide. Those who work in the prevention centers see themselves as a stopgap measure. If they can get the person through the initial problem, they then hope to arrange extended counseling.

One estimate is that an average center gets three types of calls. A third of their callers are on the dangerous edge of suicide. Another third are facing some other crisis. The final third are just looking for someone to talk to. Talking is a therapeutic preventative.

• *Fact:* A person about to commit suicide has a communication problem.

The individual's inability to express his true feelings is apparent. Ninety percent of adolescents who attempt suicide complain they cannot talk to their parents. However, we are back to the problem of the chicken and the egg. A wall of silence may not be the parents' fault. The young person may have voluntarily withdrawn into his shell. Despite loving and selfless attempts to communicate, the parents often find the youth has cut the lines. Hopefully, he will be able to find someone with whom he can talk.

- *Fact:* Suicide victims are not cowards.

Possibly no word does more to cloud the important issues. They are neither brave nor cowardly. In most cases they see no alternative to what they are about to do. Their judgment is confused. They want to live. They can't cope, but they would like help. Words such as *coward* only make it more difficult for them to seek assistance.

- *Fact:* The church's attitude is changing.

There is less feeling that suicide is the ultimate sin. Education has helped alter our concepts, and so has the immediacy of the problem. The more people we know who have done it, the more compassion we seem to develop. Seldom do denominations refuse a church burial for a suicide victim. Few pastors refuse to perform the service. Fewer people see it as the unforgivable sin. Evidence that the position is mellowing can be seen in more clergymen working as volunteers in prevention centers. Most pastors would be helpful to a family or potential victim.

- *Fact:* Parents are a significant factor.

In some suicides the dominant maternal role and the absent or silent father can be a major contributing cause. This cause, however, can be easily overemphasized. Mothers are not to be automatically blamed. Many mothers have been made to feel needlessly guilty. Many suicides have had considerate, devoted mothers. A case could also be made that strong mothers are responsible for many national leaders.

• *Fact:* Life insurance companies pay most suicides.

Companies often have a time clause of approximately two years. After this span, they normally pay in the event of suicide. If the company can prove suicide was intended when the policy was purchased, it can contest years later. In these rare cases the company argues fraud.

• *Fact:* Most medical insurance does not cover suicide cases.

The treatment of self-inflicted wounds or attempted suicide are often not paid by hospitalization policies.

• *Fact:* The anniversary of a suicide is a particularly dangerous time.

Many close loved ones are distraught as they remember the tragedy. This is a critical time, and friends should make themselves available. One teenager had himself arrested and was placed in the same cell his brother had occupied. He committed suicide just as his brother had done one year earlier.

EIGHT

HOW PEOPLE
KILL THEMSELVES
WITHOUT SUICIDE

BOB'S PARENTS WERE DEEPLY CONCERNED about his drug abuse. Twice he had taken an overdose and nearly died. He was in serious trouble with the police, and things were not improving.

Their desire to help was intense and sincere. They spent large sums of money to pay for first-class assistance. The only problem with their approach was their inability to see past the drugs. Their goal was to dry him out, to isolate him from his previous surroundings. What they could not see was that no matter where Bob went, he would still be Bob. Drugs were only a symptom of his real need. Until someone dealt with his basic personality, he would probably always have trouble.

Bob had a pounding dislike for himself. He doubted his ability and dwelt on self-pity. In his attempt to run away from himself, he turned to drugs. He had not made an overt decision to commit suicide; he just wanted to be annihilated for short periods, to escape life for a while. At some of his darkest moments, however, he didn't care whether he made it back or not.

People who work in behavioral sciences are convinced that many people are killing themselves without officially committing suicide. They find life tasteless, dull, even threatening. Desperately they look for a period of escape, and if that time period extends into eternity, they really wouldn't mind.

Escapism itself is not a bad thing. No one can stare at the sun all day; you have to look away and get some relief. An afternoon of golf, a nap, a weekend of fishing are all healthy diversions. But some people are looking for a more drastic departure. The normal releases are not enough. Eventually their form of escape will result in self-destruction without being an official suicide. Dr. Karl Menninger in his classic book *Man Against Himself* describes alcoholics and drug abusers as "chronic suicides." They destroy themselves continuously, approaching the corridors of death with mixed emotions. A military chaplain who counsels alcoholics said, "I have no doubt it is suicide. Unable to cope with life, the alcoholic is killing himself inch by inch. Despite his protests to the contrary, he knows he is dying a little bit at a time."

This attitude can be seen readily among American Indians. The Indian Health Service believes alcoholism above any other condition adversely affects Indian life in the United States. The American Indian has a suicide rate five times higher than the national average. Calvin Frederick says the problem is so acute because Indians lack something to live for. Consequently, they almost literally drown themselves in alcohol.

Many people look at life in the manner a character on television did. The police tried to frighten him into giving information. They told him other gangsters were looking for him and he soon would be dead. Without expression he asked, "How will I know the difference?" He was another of the walking dead.

Life has become too painful for thousands of people. When the tensions begin to crush them, they look for some means of escape, and they are indifferent about the ultimate effects.

These pressures begin early in life and come from different causes. Perhaps there have been too many years of continuous competition or unbroken waves of failure. Some individuals have experienced almost no accomplishments in their lives and feel it is pointless to live. Whatever the cause, their conclusion is essentially the same: Life simply is not worth it.

This in part accounts for the recent increase in youth suicide. The pressure, real and imagined, has become too much. Drugs and alcohol have become routes of escape.

Although drugs and alcohol are the most obvious

forms of nonsuicidal self-destruction, they are far from the only ones. Some hypochondriacs are self-destructive. Their hope to find something critically wrong with themselves is often a cry for help. They believe things are rougher for them than for most others. If only people could know how sick they are. They actually hope the doctor will find a serious, even terminal, illness.

In a large hospital in Detroit, a woman was scheduled for her thirteenth surgery. Something else was being removed to compensate for a mysterious pain. The previous dozen alterations had failed to restore her to acceptable health.

The hospital counselor complained. "It's obvious what is happening to this lady. She has deep personal problems that need attention. But no one wants to sit her down and try to deal with them. It's easier to schedule another operation and see if things will clear up."

As we have suggested, many suicide victims visit a physician shortly before attempting self-destruction, perhaps hoping to find a physical basis for their depression. They have the physical ability, but not the spirit, to live.

Some individuals on life-sustaining medicine will play Russian roulette. A diabetic may repeatedly forget his insulin. He resents being dependent on the drug and wants to tempt his illness. He realizes the risk involved, yet he is halfway willing to take that chance. After all, he figures, life on pills and shots is only barely worth living anyway. He would probably never commit suicide, but if he happens to die, he would not really mind.

In other cases, cancer patients have been told they have to return to the hospital for more treatment. They calculate the expense, the discomfort, and the prospects. They make the decision no longer to fight it, and cancer takes its course.

Another form of self-destruction is voluntary starvation. The person who reaches a crisis level and simply doesn't care to go on may start to eat less. There isn't much fight left in his system. He does not want to shoot or hang himself, and yet he really doesn't care to go on. As the body weakens, the individual withdraws into his own psychological shell. He is hard to reach, difficult to motivate. Eventually he merely expires.

A decade ago, the college-age daughter of a famous movie star died this way. One day she resigned from life, restricted herself to her room, and refused to eat or communicate. After she dwindled to less than one hundred pounds, death came. From all indications, the incident was as much a suicide as that produced by a gunshot wound.

Dr. Hilde Bruch, professor of psychiatry at Baylor College of Medicine, believes this type of death is on the increase. The practice is particularly rising among girls in high school and college who are from economically privileged families. Many are suffering from what Dr. Bruch calls *anorexia nervosa,* a desire for perfection mingled with anxieties over the injustices of life. In the middle of this confusion, they become obsessed with the imperfections in their own bodies. They stop eating and eventually starve to death.

As odd as the problem may seem, it appears to be growing. One of the most publicized cases concerned Stephanie Powers, written up in *Reader's Digest,* October, 1977. Neither she nor her family could overcome the combination of endless activity and growing inability to eat. Finally, this child from a financially secure home starved herself to death.

Another form of the same problem involves a sudden desire to overeat. A person begins to increase his diet at a noticeable pace. He continues to gain weight even though he has been warned of the possible effects on his heart.

Obviously not everyone who is overweight is suicidal. But for some it is a conscious (or possibly unconscious) attempt to annihilate themselves. In a few cases, people have felt locked into a job they cannot escape. Unable to adapt, they decide life does not really matter anyway. They intentionally deface themselves and care little whether they live or die.

Social scientists are not sure what is happening on the nation's highways, but they are convinced that people's attitudes and temperaments seriously affect what a car does. The number of vehicular suicides may be extremely high. But more difficult to determine are the number of careless ones.

We are not talking about the typical reckless driver or thrill seeker who wants to see how close he can come to cement bridges. We are now discussing an entirely different breed. Suppose a driver leaves home after a particularly painful fight with his wife.

FACTS ABOUT SUICIDE

He is on his way to a job he desperately hates. He is depressed; life seems hopeless. Soon the accelerator is pushing seventy and he is buzzing through intersections. When another car comes slamming into his side, he doesn't care.

Technically, it isn't suicide. He wasn't looking for a way to die. And yet, it was more than a casual accident. His state of mind was uncaring.

A man fails to negotiate a sharp turn. A woman loses a race with a train. Sometimes they are normal accidents, but at other times the facts are more complicated.

Francine Klagburn, in her book *Youth and Suicide,* calls for more education about drivers' emotions. She insists that recognizing our emotional condition is as important as being able to identify road signs and signal lights.

Psychiatrist Norman Tabachnick did research into fatal accidents in the Los Angeles area. He discovered 25 percent of fatal accidents involved depressed drivers who had earlier expressed feelings of self-destruction and fantasies about death.

The other 75 percent were under no particular pressures, and still they were involved in fatal accidents. The statistics do not prove which group is more dangerous. They do demonstrate, however, that a large number of depressed people are driving tons of steel along the highways.

Robert Litman reports a sizable number of "equivocal" deaths, those that may be suicide but no one can say for certain. Yet, there are enough clues to make the investigator wonder.

A man in the Midwest became frustrated. His job was insecure and he faced a court sentence. One day he abruptly hijacked a small plane with its pilot and copilot and forced them to fly to the outskirts of a large city. Once they landed there, he made odd demands and threatened to shoot his hostages. First he wanted to be flown to this country and then to that one. Yet he did not order them to leave the ground. In his heated actions, he fired two shots into the side of the craft. The police then quickly moved in and shot the hijacker to death.

Did this man commit suicide? Was he really hoping someone would shoot him? As it turned out, he hurt no one but himself, his family, and friends. Certainly he has to be listed as an "equivocal" death. His motives died with him.

Authorities on the subject are convinced that many who rob and murder are, in reality, committing suicide. They may even hold a hostage in such a position as to allow a policeman to shoot—they want to be killed. Yet their deaths will never be listed as suicides.

Some of this nation's most famous gangsters knew full well what their future held. They did not expect to get away forever, nor did they intend to have the police take them alive. They were making a date with a bullet. The basic difference was they wanted someone else to pull the trigger.

NINE

THE YOUTH
EPIDEMIC

A BOILING POT OF PRESSURE AND CHANGE exists inside thousands of young people, and occasionally it blows up. Many young people don't know how to reduce the steam, and sometimes they can't keep the lid on.

The number of youth suicides in America is increasing. In the past twenty years, suicides in the 16-24 age group have tripled. These are all types of youth: dropouts, drug users, and straight-A students who have never failed at anything.

A mother and father in an Ivy League town were shocked when they found their seventeen-year-old daughter unconscious in her bed. She had taken an overdose of sleeping pills and was only partly alive.

Their girl had never given them a moment of trouble. She did everything right and was a popular student. Only now did they realize Ann had hostilities and frustrations that she never expressed before.

Youth suicide is not limited to the high-school and college-age. Today and every day of the year two youths under sixteen will end their lives. These figures do not include those young people who die from "reckless" suicide—young people who are bored, depressed, and don't care if they live or die. They drive their cars as if there were no tomorrow or take drugs as if they are trying to see how close they can get to death. If they die, their death will not be listed as an official suicide. But they certainly exhibited destructive behavior and possibly even a death wish.

The specific causes of increased youth suicides are hard to determine. We are sure of a number of contributing factors. The large number of broken homes adds to the feelings of insecurity and doubts about love. Seventy-one percent of youths who commit suicide come from divorced homes. Many cannot work out their feelings about the change in their homes, and often they feel personally responsible for the split.

The enormous pressure from the educational process is crippling to some young people, and yet others thrive on it. Confusion over shifting standards leaves some youths completely torn. Some young people commit suicide after having intercourse because of the tremendous guilt. Some are unsure about their role in life. In the process of growing up, they may have lost a healthy self-respect, and they consider themselves the dandruff of the world.

Drugs do play a role in the number of youth suicides, but the exact extent is difficult to determine. Some authorities believe drugs are involved in half of the adolescent suicides. But which came first, the chicken or the egg? Are some youth so depressed and suicidal that they turn to drug abuse? Or are they fairly stable until the drugs diminish their ability to think? Many young people see drugs as an opportunity to live and die at the same time. The drugs allow them to escape life and its pressures; consequently, they often take them. Yet drugs let them return to life for whatever it offers. In this game of escape, a number of youth venture too far too often. Sometimes they don't make it back. At other times, they never intended to come back. The difference between an overdose and suicide can be paper-thin.

Young people, despite their cries of independence, are, like all of us, vulnerable to suggestions and influences. When suicides are romanticized in our culture, a spark ignites that results in many self-inflicted deaths. The deaths of Marilyn Monroe, Ernest Hemingway, Judy Garland, Freddie Prinze, Janis Joplin, Sylvia Plath, or Japanese author Yukio Mishima all took their toll. People say to themselves, "If he can't make it with all he has, what chance do I have?" The publicity surrounding these suicides set off a chain of sudden deaths.

Sociologist David Phillips of the University of California in San Diego has gathered some facts. He studied five large California newspapers to check the publicity they gave to "famous" suicides. Then he checked the records of vehicle fatalities. Three days after the publicity of a notable suicide, the number of vehicle fatalities rose by 30 percent. The rest of the week, it remained 9 percent above normal.

Because of our effect on each other, there are those who are afraid to discuss suicide. Why bring up such a morbid subject? Talking about it will only cause more people to end their lives.

One man was scheduled to speak for a week on a college campus. His topic on the fourth day was announced as "Suicide." A school administrator came to him privately. "Speak on anything you want," he said, "sex, war, even communism. But leave suicide alone. It will only cause a rash of them on campus."

The educator's apprehension is understandable, but his energy may be misspent. The important factor is not whether suicide is discussed, but how.

The topic of suicide suffers from a communication problem. Most youths who commit suicide are trying to communicate. Possibly because of their own problems, they cannot express their desperate hurt. Killing themselves is the final message. "See, I really was hurting." At last they got it across.

Knowledge is better than ignorance. Sharing is better than seething. If the environment says suicide is something we do not discuss, what are the victim's options? He feels drawn toward it. He wonders about it. And he has to bottle up these feelings, because talking about suicide is taboo.

Larry was a Christian in his early twenties. A major concern in his life was to follow Jesus Christ as a committed disciple. He tried to examine every aspect of his thoughts, his motives, and his actions in a spiritual context.

He was single and found sex becoming an overriding factor in his mind. Yet he fought it and then felt doubly guilty for even thinking about it. But there was no one for Larry to talk to. Sex was a subject that received a few sneers from the pulpit, but nice people didn't talk about it.

Larry became so overwrought with his "burden of sin" that he started to consider suicide. But since nice people also didn't discuss suicide, he was trapped again. One evening he was found standing on the edge of a high-rise roof. He threatened to jump but did not really want to. Larry was trying to find some way of letting people know he hurt.

Now people are willing to talk to him. They discuss anything he wants. He has spent the past fifteen years in and out of mental hospitals and clinics.

A pastor in the Midwest took seriously the rumors he heard about high-school students who were discussing the merits of suicide. He made it a point to befriend these youths individually, without mentioning suicide. Eventually, each brought up the subject. One day, to his complete surprise, all four showed up at his office. They had compared notes and wanted to discuss it together. After several sessions, the two who were not Christians invited Christ into their lives.

To discover how much people want to talk about suicide, tell everyone you are writing a book on the subject! Many have a relative who tried it or did it. They have always wondered about this or that. Perhaps during the last couple years they have considered it themselves. People are more curious about suicide than we may have thought.

The two hundred suicide prevention centers across the United States are vivid evidence. Their phones ring continuously. The center in Los Angeles gets twenty thousand calls a month. In a medium-sized city like Omaha, the number is two thousand. People want to talk about it.

But where can a young person go to discuss his problem? Some are boxed in and do not feel free to bring it up. Traditionally, local ministers have been a good source for counseling, but many youths have avoided them when it comes to suicide. Churches often speak of suicide only in terms of condemnation. Hopefully, ministers will do more to demonstrate a helpful spirit—to show they do understand and would like to help. For many young people, pastors and chaplains are more easily accessible than psychologists, psychiatrists, or even school counselors.

Parents are often embarrassed when their child seeks counseling. They take it personally. It seems to point up their failures. We need to be glad that, if our child needed someone to talk to, he had enough sense to find a listening ear.

TEN

STALKING
THE AGED

SUICIDE AMONG THE YOUNG is a spectacular subject. It vibrates with intrigue, drama, and shock.
"How could they do it when they had so much to live
for?"

Just as tragic, however, is the large number of
elderly who decide to end it all. In recent years, the
suicide rate among the middle-aged and elderly has
grown sharply. Today the problem is a constant
concern to those who work among geriatrics.

If the elderly suicide fits a pattern, it runs along
these lines. He is alone, fairly isolated, without close
relatives or children. He faces a job crisis and is
bothered by ill health, real or imagined.

We use *he* in this instance because the rate of male

suicides in this age bracket is remarkably higher than female. In England the rate of male suicides over sixty is five times that of women. The United States has a ratio of ten to one.

The chaplain of a retirement village expressed his urgent interest. "Suicide is a real and vital concern of our aged," he said. The two causes he gives cannot be ignored: depression and uselessness. Our society, both Christian and secular, needs to reevaluate its attitude toward the retiree. Many simply do not have enough reason to live. Their role in society has often become meaningless, and they would rather leave than bear the hardship.

It is important to recognize a distinction. There are not more suicides among the elderly simply because their number is greater. The increase is a percentage: More elderly per hundred thousand are calling it quits.

A retired missionary who killed himself a few years ago is fairly typical of the problem. He had served almost fifty years in Africa. As a single man, he was always surrounded by coworkers and nationals. His work load was heavy, and there was little time to feel sorry for himself.

The mission board forced him to retire at seventy and brought him back to the United States. His future consisted of failing health and idleness. He was not a thrilling speaker, and few groups asked for his services. The change was too much. He had no intention of spending his last years in painful uselessness. He tied a rope to a beam and ended it.

Many reaching old age feel like the psalmist,

"And now, in my old age, don't set me aside. Don't forsake me now when my strength is failing" (Ps. 71: 9).

Many people feel as if everything is falling apart. They do not want a dull, tasteless, even painful life. The psalmist goes on, "And now that I am old and gray, don't forsake me. Give me time to tell this new generation (and their children, too) about all your mighty miracles" (Ps. 71: 18).

Will was in his eighties when I met him. He had a good spirit and a halting memory. His large frame was starting to bend and ache. Will's advice was crisp and telling—"Don't grow old." The way he said it, I knew he was sincere.

The increase in suicides begins to climb sharply among forty-year-olds. This steady increase continues until seventy and then tapers off.

Social isolation is one of the greatest contributing factors to self-destruction among the elderly according to studies of both Durkheim and Sainsbury. Health and economics play a large role in causing isolation. Some people can no longer afford to keep up with their former social outlets. Others are too sick and restricted to get out easily.

A number of Christian groups and churches have become aware of this problem and are moving to help. Often they are turning to innovative solutions.

A large Baptist church in Washington, D.C., has developed a program called "meals on heels." Every day a free dinner is supplied for those who can walk there. The church feels a healthy hot meal is one you have to go and get. Approaches like this give many elderly a bright spot every day and encourages social interchange.

Some churches have formed local action groups. Instead of shelving the elderly, they put them to work and use their skills. Programs such as these tell the retiree he is still necessary.

A few churches have hired some elderly for part-time work such as doing hospital visitation or giving Bible studies. The payment is a supplement to his Social Security check. Some churches could hire six to ten people.

Dr. Justus Shifferers has reported the situation accurately when he said, "The true tragedy of old age is not poverty but loneliness" (*The Older People in Your Life*). The seriousness of the problem is verified by the number of suicides.

In the immediate future, the elderly population will continue to multiply. People born in 1910 in the United States had a life expectancy of 48. Females born in 1980 can expect to live until they are 80. If major breakthroughs occur against cancer or heart disease, life expectancy in 2030 could be 120. Our society will change its attitude toward the elderly because it must.

If loneliness is the most serious problem among the elderly suicides, certainly health is second. In all age groups illness has been found to be an important factor in self-destruction. However, in the group over sixty years old, physical illness was the most common precipitating factor.

Physical illness prevents many conflicts that lead to suicide. Some of the elderly are afraid they cannot bear the pain. They face treatment for cancer or an otherwise debilitating sickness. Rather than combat what they feel is hopeless agony, they decide to terminate.

Others are fearful of death itself and consequently commit suicide. Their dread is that they will not face death well. Rather than humiliate themselves later, they dictate their own exit.

Frequently elderly people select death over financial burden. They see hospital and doctor bills eroding their savings or placing a shackle on their relatives. Some elderly have flatly refused medical attention, because they had so little income.

Marriage also has a definite effect on the elderly and suicide. Those who are single, widowed, or divorced have a higher percentage of self-destruction. In some areas, the rate is twice that of those who are married. Of those left alone, the divorced presently are the most likely to commit suicide. These figures seem to again bear out the necessity for others. Those who become isolated, for whatever reason, often find it more difficult to cope. Most people left to themselves don't make out well. God spelled out the principle early in man's existence. "And the Lord God said, 'It isn't good for man to be alone; I will make a companion for him, a helper suited to his needs'" (Gen. 2:18).

One of the saddest cries in the Bible is from the psalmist who prayed:

> Don't turn away from me in this time of my distress. Bend down your ear and give me

speedy answers, for my days disappear like
smoke. My health is broken and my heart is
sick; it is trampled like grass and is withered.
My food is tasteless, and I have lost my appe-
tite. I am reduced to skin and bones because of
all my groaning and despair. I am like a vul-
ture in a far-off wilderness, or like an owl
alone in the desert. I lie awake, lonely as a
solitary sparrow on the roof.

Psalm 102:2-7

With the problems of isolation, health, and
uselessness, depression has to be a natural result.
Millions of the elderly manage to avoid depression,
but many others cannot.

When the older person concludes life is hopeless,
he follows a particular trend in suicide. Generally he
selects a violent, quick method of death. Guns and
hangings are among the most frequently used.

The significance of the methods should not be
overlooked. Their choice is definite proof these individuals are not seeking sympathy. Guns are not a
gamble with death. The person who uses a gun has
no illusions of someone finding him in time. His
primary goal is to end his life.

Sometimes we picture an elderly gentleman coming to the end of his days and calmly deciding to cut
them short. It sounds like a pastoral scene of peaceful exit. Most of the time the exact opposite is true.
If he could, he would choose to live, but his circumstances are too overbearing. He is alone; his
health is short; and he has lost a meaningful place in

society. He feels there is nothing to live for.

Large numbers of these lives could be saved and given years of enjoyment if some caring person or group would reach out to them.

ELEVEN

DIFFERENT TYPES
OF SUICIDE

IT WOULD BE SAFE TO SAY the number of suicides in the United States is extremely high. The figures we publish are the bare minimum. The low official statistics are basically an attempt to be kind.

Imagine what happens when a body is discovered. The police and the coroner see evidence that suicide is a prospect. They also realize the devastating consequences if this death is ruled to have been self-inflicted. The family will suffer decades of agony. The insurance company may delay payment on the policy. Children, parents, partners are all in for a long road of personal problems.

Local officials are eager to be kind, even in metropolitan areas. Many set out determined to prove it was not a suicide. They will grab at any clue or slightest hint that it was an accident. If a note has been left, naturally there is little choice. But if there is any hope of pronouncing a verdict of accidental or natural death, they usually take it.

There are drawbacks, however, to this type of generosity. To begin with, we have no accurate way of estimating how many people kill themselves every year. We guess thirty-to-thirty-five thousand. The correct figures might be one hundred thousand or more.

The importance of knowing is more than a morbid curiosity. By accurately understanding what is happening, specialists in the field can map a strategy to prevent suicides. But they need to get good data on the how, when, why, and how often of suicides. The more they know, the more they can help.

In some cases, the family is done a disservice by pretending the death was accidental. Often the relatives suspect the truth. They have watched the victim's conflicts and heard his threats. Now that he is dead, the family naturally wonders. They may like to talk about it, maybe resolve some of their feelings. But everyone assures them no, a suicide didn't happen—they should just forget about it.

The fact is, they need someone to talk to, but all their efforts are rejected. They need to open their emotions and express what they think. The evidence would relieve their minds and possibly allow them to face up to the truth.

To help wrestle with the mysteries of suicide, Dr.

Shneidman has developed a "psychological autopsy." When the physical evidence is lacking and yet suicide is suspected, this method could prove helpful.

The psychologist studies the background leading up to the death. What pressures did he face? What changes were taking place? What thoughts or threats had he shared with others?

Dr. Theodore Curphey, Los Angeles chief medical examiner-coroner, has begun using the procedure. He may invite trained authorities in suicide to investigate a death and recommend a ruling. The team is not out to prove a suicide. They may be able to disprove one. Either way, their findings are often a warm comfort to the family.

Those who commit suicide come in a large array of personalities and intentions. Some choose to die rather than spend a year in jail. Others choose not to live as an invalid. Some cannot face debts. Their reasons are complex. In an attempt to get a handle on the subject, Durkheim divided victims into three broad categories, and these divisions are helpful. I have reworked them into popular language. We need to remember that they overlap.

• The first group is the *internal crisis*. An individual in this group has difficulty coping largely because of feelings of inadequacy. His external life may be doing fine; possibly he has a good job and a fine family, but still he has trouble holding on. He feels inferior, and outside circumstances cannot convince him otherwise. He has a bruised or shattered ego. Normally he has faced a series of setbacks, particularly as a youth. He may have spent years struggling to prevent total failure. The thought of suicide has crossed his mind often, but so far he has fought back successfully.

Worn down and internally defeated, he is a prime candidate for a disaster. Something eventually comes along and jars his delicate balance. The catalyst may be small, even insignificant. A neighbor complains about a dog, a boss becomes impatient, the car breaks down. During a period when he is particularly down on himself, anything could be tragic. Unfortunately, the survivors will always remember the incident that triggered the suicide. In fact, the final straw might have had little to do with the death.

Ernie shot himself soon after his girlfriend told him to no longer come around. She carried the stigma of the death, but it in fact was not hers. Ernie could have ended his life over a rejection by the armed services or a failure on an entrance exam. He was unhappy with himself and doubted his ability to cope. Losing a girlfriend represented another setback he felt unequipped to handle.

Life can be compared with a tent. If a tent has 10-12 pegs securing the ropes, it is probably secure. When the wind and rain come, the canvas may flap a little, possibly even lean, but it will hold. Sometimes we lose a few pegs, but the tent still does the job. But if we are missing five or six pegs, it's a different story.

Most of us are stabilized by several stakes in life. But some people are down to barely a few. They are often loners, have few hobbies, or suffer from poor self-esteem. Each day is more of a threat than a promise. Someday a storm may come along, and the tent won't hold. Maybe just a gentle wind will leave it in a heap.

● A second category is *drastic external change.* A person in this group experiences an overwhelming shift in his life. Those who leaped from buildings during the Depression are representative. Some advocates of euthanasia are included in this category. Often he is a person with a strong ego who is determined to handle his own fate.

Recently an article appeared on the front page of the newspaper concerning a former professor. He was eighty and suffering from a miserable, crippling disease. He made arrangements to visit an elderly friend in another state. He spent a week with his comrade and told him what he intended to do. They enjoyed hours of memories and a few drinks.

The friend made no attempt to dissuade the old professor. The next morning he was found dead with an empty pill bottle by his bed. He had no lack of self-esteem. He simply knew what he wanted and decided to select his own exit.

Those who select suicide during torture and physical threat are also part of this group. Many who killed themselves in concentration camps decided to steal fate away from their captors.

Ward's suicide presented peculiar problems to a psychological autopsy team. He apparently had no difficulties. A business executive, his career was still booming, and at sixty, his health appeared excellent. Over the years, Ward had collected many interests and pursued several hobbies. He and his wife of thirty-five years were highly compatible.

One Saturday he played golf with three of his many friends. He shot a good score, had a drink, and returned to his plush home. Everyone reported him to be in a buoyant spirit. In his den he pointed a rifle at his head and pulled the trigger.

If ever there seemed an atypical suicide, Ward was it. However, the investigating team discovered something even his wife didn't know. A doctor had told him he would soon lose his vision. Ward decided to control his own fate.

• The third group is distinctive. It is composed of those who commit suicide for a purpose or cause. Durkheim called this category *altruistic*. These are deaths demanded by society or religion.

Some women have killed themselves rather than lose their virginity. Christians have ended their lives for fear of forsaking the faith under persecution. Tribesmen follow tradition and die after a humiliation. Hara-kiri is an example of suicide under social pressure. The wife of a Japanese general reportedly was irate because her husband did not kill himself. She couldn't be expected to live with a defeated soldier. When she arrived to pick up his body, she thoroughly derided him for still being in it.

The most famous suicides of the past fifty years have been the Japanese kamikaze pilots. Despite rumors, these young men were neither drugged nor tied into their planes. As Japan's military strength slipped away, hundreds of flyers volunteered to crash into American vessels. Why? They were not threatened with harm. Their belief in reincarnation did make the decision somewhat easier; however, as some of the volunteers have since testified, their fear of death was real. Each overcame that fear with dedication to their homeland and emperor.

Cheyenne Indians often turned to suicide during their days of power and freedom. Whenever a warrior lost prestige with the tribe, he would seek to end his life. If he appeared to be a coward in battle or during a hunt, the pressure became immense. He would then kill himself to regain his honor.

Among African tribes, self-destruction became a custom. A person could commit suicide in order to get even with someone else. If the tribe believed someone caused the suicide, the perpetrator was forced to end his own life in the same way.

People do not fall neatly into categories. But these groupings can help us begin to understand some of the causes.

PART THREE
THE POTENTIAL SUICIDE

TWELVE

HOW CAN
WE TELL?

"YOU COULD SEE HE WAS THINKING about it. John had a lot of problems. He was deep into drugs and the police were hassling him. He couldn't find any way out."

The speaker was a high-school girl who wasn't surprised at her friend's suicide. She had seen the raging storm for weeks before John turned a shotgun on himself.

Not all of the signs are as clear. Even a professional counselor cannot predict with certainty when someone will attempt to end his life. There is special danger in becoming amateur analysts. Our imagination gets the best of us, and soon we see the marks of suicide in everyone. We cannot emphasize too strongly how dangerous this is. Most people will never attempt to end their own lives.

If someone comes home after work and says something odd, there is no reason to panic. He may say, "Boy, some days I wonder what life is all about." Or there might be a sudden drop in your daughter's grades. These are not reasons to rush them to the mental health clinic. When studying a subject as heavy as suicide, we tend to overdramatize the material.

Normally the action is a result of a culmination of events. The important signs to watch for are patterns rather than incidents, a collection of traits rather than an outburst.

One significant pattern to be aware of is speech. If an individual's conversation centers continuously on withdrawing, quitting, and hopelessness or has a tone of despair, particularly about himself and his immediate surroundings, it should act as a danger signal. When someone says he can't take his job any longer and he doesn't think he can find another one, he is making a boxed-in statement. If he does not like his job and plans to apply at the National Bank, the coloring is entirely different. He is then speaking of disappointment and hope. But statements of ultimate despair can point to a problem.

The first time he says it may be a simple overstatement. All of us exaggerate. But if he hangs onto the pattern, a pressure head may be building.

Other statements may seem aimless but are definitely indicative of depression. "Life doesn't really make much sense, does it?" Or, "I just feel like a misfit no matter what I do." A famous writer of fiction who killed himself supposedly called life "just a cruel joke."

Anyone who develops these patterns may or may not be suicidal, but he certainly is hurting. If the symptom persists, he should not be ignored. The fact that he verbalizes it is probably an overt cry for help. His friends will do well to respond with positive conversation.

The apostle Paul sometimes felt the terrific pressures of life. His experience was common to ours. "We are hard pressed on every side, but not crushed; perplexed, but not in despair; persecuted, but not abandoned; struck down, but not destroyed" (2 Cor. 4: 8-9). He was pushed to the brink of despair but not over it. Like most of us, he could understand the person who feels overwhelmed.

Another set of phrases may be more urgent. "I doubt I'll still be around by Christmas"; or, "The kids would be a lot happier without me." Even if this person is not serious about suicide, he is serious about something. If his conversations are taking this route, he has an acute problem. It would be unwise to ignore him. Dr. Shneidman reminds us that this type of statement can be the most telling.

A third set of sentences are the pointed ones. "I'm going to kill myself someday." "My dad committed suicide; maybe it runs in our family." "I don't plan to be here tomorrow."

Folklore has told us to ignore these people. It claimed those who talked about suicide never did it. Today we know this is not true. We need to respond immediately to an alarm like this.

The person who develops those speech patterns is basically saying one thing: "I need help!" He finds himself in a situation with which he cannot cope. He sees no solutions. But the fact that he talks indicates how much he would like some answers. Someone needs to step in and kindly suggest alternatives, to show him there is a way to solve his problem.

Along with a change in an individual's speech may also come a new set of actions. His physical behavior could take one of two extremes. He may suddenly become slow and listless, showing no enthusiasm. He might begin to walk slower or allow himself a dumpy disposition. He goes through the motions but has lost any fighting spirit.

The other extreme is to become reckless. He drinks with defiance or provokes arguments. Suddenly there is a car accident that he made little or no effort to avoid.

Some potential victims develop a pattern of giving things away—possibly an old afghan that belonged to grandmother, or maybe an antique car he had been working on. These actions are accompanied with statements like "You keep this, I won't need it anymore." Not everyone who gives something away is suicidal. But as part of a larger pattern it becomes significant.

Or a suicidal individual might become overly concerned with funeral arrangements. Maybe he will pick out a casket and talk more about how he wants to be buried. Some will check into their insurance policies or will. In isolation, these acts can be normal and productive. We all should take these good sound steps. But if his other actions are odd, there could be reason for genuine concern.

Often a suicidal person is facing harsh changes in his circumstances. We have already mentioned stress over employment. Possibly he has been transferred to a job he feels incapable of handling. He dreads it every day but thinks he cannot change the situation. Maybe a new boss has been appointed, and he expects to get fired in the near future.

Marital stress is frequently a contribution to suicide. The press has suggested actor Freddie Prinze may have ended his life as a result of a separation. Change presents conflict for most of us. Some changes make it particularly difficult for us to cope.

More than one person has killed himself at the prospect of a pending operation if the outcome didn't appear hopeful. Patients can be afraid they will become physically restricted, or they might be convinced the disease will end in death anyway. Such persons need all the positive input they can get.

It is especially important during these stress situations to be honest with the individual. A person under stress often turns people off if he feels they are telling lies to try to cheer him up. Phrases like "Look, I know it's going to be tough" are more beneficial than those that attempt to hide reality. Frankness coupled with hope is the healthiest combination.

The potential victim is already suspicious. Any

friend or counselor who loses his credibility will only drive a difficult wedge into the relationship. Assurances that everything will work out fine are too sugarcoated.

If there is one emotion that covers most potential victims, it is depression. We all seem to get the blues sometimes, but their case has become critical. No longer a passing feeling, depression settles in and permeates their lives as smoke saturates clothing.

Depression is usually connected with a feeling of worthlessness. The person is convinced that he has nothing to offer, that he cannot do anything correctly. This lack of love for himself results in a belief that no one else loves him either.

It is obvious to those around him that he is wrong. We can think of a host of things he does well. But these are beside the point. He has sessions of extremely poor judgment. These spells may come in short spurts or last for days. The important point is how he feels about himself, and at this stage it is not good.

Jesus Christ laid down a concrete principle when he told us to love our neighbor as ourselves (Matt. 19:19). A break in this cycle, for whatever reason, is harmful to the entire man.

At this stage of depression, the last thing the person needs is to be chewed out. "Snap out of it and stop acting like a baby" may be fatal. In some people, this shock treatment could be helpful, but for most it is taking an extreme chance.

A teenager had talked to his girl friend several times about the possibility of ending his life. She became tired of the morbid, frightening talk and finally told him, "Why don't you stop this and just go ahead and do it?"

She doubtless thought she was doing him a favor, hoping he would snap out of his moodiness.

For the young man, the words were murderous. He was now in a terrible dilemma. Immediately he went to a high bridge and began to pace. She had questioned his honesty and courage. He could no longer face her unless he at least tried to kill himself. If he continued to live, he could not discuss his deepest fears with her. She had ridiculed him, and yet he needed her. He had been pushed into a corner and saw no alternative. This position of making someone feel there are no other answers is what most needs to be avoided.

Well-meaning Christians sometimes try to be helpful by making the individual deal with a sinful situation in his life. They think that by being blunt with the potential victim he will face up to his godless attitude, repent, and pull out of his mire.

Granted, sin may well be involved in the situation, but the poorest time to try to make a person change is while he is contemplating suicide. He already considers himself bad news. If someone calls him a sinner, it only confirms what he feared all along. Further charges could be terminal.

If the potential victim wants to discuss a sin, then by all means listen; he may need to get it out. We can do him an excellent service by listening. But remember, the depressed person does not need more to be depressed about.

THE POTENTIAL SUICIDE

Depression is a funny animal. It is somewhat like trying to train a wild beast. The minute you think it is under control, the animal will turn on you. The person who suffers from severe depression may come out of it for periods, apparently successfully. However, many people commit suicide after coming out of a depression spell. During their darkest moments, they may have lacked even enough ambition to take their own lives. After the clouds have shifted, the victim can think a little better—but not clearly. He is resolved to no longer live in the dank well of depression. Therefore, he ends his life to finally escape the depths of despair.

If any of this fails to make sense to you, remember it is watertight reasoning to the victim. He is thinking the best he can, and this is what he often comes up with.

Depression that reaches the critical stage is hard to handle. Time, patience, and persistence are essential to achieve ultimate healing. People in situations in which they feel inadequate and dependent often choose a desperate exit.

Ben was involved in a difficult marriage. His wife was clearly dominant, and he seethed under her command. The relationship was an insult to his manhood. He could not fight her for the leadership spot, and yet he felt strongly that it was his.

The situation was intolerable to him. Neither divorce nor separation were compatible with his beliefs. Every day his feelings of self-worth were growing smaller and smaller. Ben saw no livable way to cope with the problem. He saw death as a solution.

There are many such people living in locked environments. Often hospital patients cannot stand giving the total control of their lives to others. One is placed in an abbreviated gown, poked, punched, fed, and given a minimum of choices. Sometimes the staff is gruff and impertinent. Occasionally a patient will throw himself out the window. More often he will merely give up, eat little, and soon expire.

It is easy to see why convicts hang themselves. They have been degraded, confined, and completely dominated. Their future seems bleak in prison and dismal outside.

If the key emotion to most suicides is depression, the key prospect is hopelessness. It is one thing to be oppressed with trouble. It is critical if the person cannot imagine any way out. One person says, "Tomorrow is going to be a tough day. I will probably get fired." He has a real problem. The second person says, "I will probably get fired. There isn't anything else I can do." The second man is desperate.

Job's wife looked him over and came up with a hopeless conclusion. She recommended he curse God and die. Hopefully, we will be able to give more constructive aid to people in despair. But Mrs. Job expresses the agony many relatives and friends face. The person who wants to end his life can be a massive heartache to everyone around him. The temptation may be for everyone to give up.

We discuss some of the reasons behind suicide so we might be better able to help. Beyond this, there is little point in fixing causes. To blame parents, wives, employers, or institutions has scarce value in assisting the victim. Often accusations only degenerate into bitterness. Incrimination and hostilities are counterproductive.

The real problem is how we can help. How can we inject hope into a terrible situation?

Dr. Shneidman insists no special equipment or talent is necessary to help. The basic ingredients are sharp eyes and ears, good intuition, a pinch of wisdom, an ability to act appropriately, and a commitment to the person.

THIRTEEN

HOW CAN
I GET HELP
FOR HIM?

PEOPLE ARE NOT CAKE MIXES. We can't pour a box of ingredients into a bowl, add two eggs and milk, and create a life. Human beings are dynamic, and no one can predict with certainty which way they will turn. Helping people is as much art as science. The guidelines that are available will work with many, but certainly not with everyone.

Whether the person is a relative, friend, or client, one cardinal rule applies: *Always take a suicide threat seriously.* Even if the individual has no intention of ending his life, he is crying for help. When someone shuts him off with a remark like, "Oh, why don't you grow up?" the problem intensifies. The potential victim just said, "I'm hurting," and someone told him in effect, "Ah, shut up."

This sort of response pushes the person to one of two choices. Either he must internalize his feelings and be quiet, or else he has to find another way to express himself. He may find a line of communication in another person or in an action. Hopefully, when one person turns him off, he will find someone else. But there comes a point at which he feels he has run out of time, and then he decides to end it all.

When someone talks about terminating himself, he is setting off an alarm. An emergency exists. The person who cares about him needs to find out what kind of emergency and at what stage it is.

The best way to evaluate the situation is to get the person talking. Don't act panicky or startled. Most people *do not* commit suicide, so relax. The person wanted to get someone's attention, and he has. He will probably be fairly cooperative. Let him know you care and would like to listen.

Suicide prevention centers and professional counselors have developed certain skills in questioning. Their experience suggests certain guidelines. Dr. Shneidman recommends we first determine where the person is in his suicidal thought, especially if he is talking over the phone. Appropriate questions might be, "How long have you thought about doing this?" Has he drawn up definite plans in his mind? Does he have a weapon or drug with him, or has he selected one?

The counselor does not want to suggest any means to him. But in a subtle way, try to determine the stage of the crisis. What is the lethal risk?

If you are convinced the risk is not immediate, you have time to talk. Your questions need to be understanding and accepting. You need to express, "I care, I want to listen, I intend to help." If he doubts your sincerity, the conversation may be aborted.

Ask open-ended questions that allow the person broad freedom in expressing himself. "How long have you felt this way?" "What bothers you the most?" "What would you really like to do?" Agree with him when you can. Be extremely positive. But don't lie to him. If he senses an insincerity, he may feel all the more betrayed.

It is important to remember that practically no one is 100 percent suicidal. If you can help lower his feelings now, there is hope. What you feel will be transmitted to the individual. Your attitude should be concerned but not despondent.

A healthy vocabulary will be a genuine asset. Phrases about life, living, and happiness can be contagious. A warm and radiant smile will help. Give the person the feeling that even in hardship he can feel content.

If he talks about injustices and disappointments that are desperate, don't be afraid to agree. Credibility is essential. But be sure you guide the conversation to positive hope as soon as it is practical.

As he allows, point the conversation toward his strengths: his favorite sport, hobby, accomplishment. If he resists, don't push him. But at least plant a mental reminder—there really are some good things to live for. If he rejects the subject or denies his ability, it at least has rekindled some thoughts.

In most cases, there is one approach to avoid. Do not try to argue the relative merits of life over death. The last thing he needs is an abrasive argument. He may have convinced himself death is a peaceful, loving contrast to his present world. His logic is probably shaky. If he is presented with positive life-giving suggestions, the arguments against suicide should take care of themselves.

A Christian youth was sharing his suicidal thoughts loosely with a friend. He explained his logic this way. "If I continue to stumble through life, I'll continue to mess up. God is disappointed in me, and I keep on sinning. If I end my life quickly, I just commit one sin and then it is all over. Then God is happy, I'm happy, and we spend eternity in peaceful bliss."

The friend obviously didn't know what to say. Finally he just blurted out, "The whole thing's sick."

As illogical as this youth's reasoning seemed, it made perfectly good sense to him. He enjoyed pushing the proposition on others because he was confident of its soundness. His desire to kill himself grew with each person's inability to refute him. The only things that dissuaded him were more personal appeals.

It does no good to win an argument and lose the person.

Another positive approach is to get the individual talking about his family, wife or husband, and children. They often represent sparks of hope and light

to him. If he immediately reacts with hostility to a
certain member, avoid that one and talk about the
others.

As we have mentioned elsewhere, children suffer
terribly in the aftermath of a suicide. The potential
victim seldom understands this. He pictures his
family as happy and prosperous, being taken care of
by someone else. He may even imagine they have
warm, compassionate feelings toward their deceased relative.

He needs to be reminded that this is almost never
the case. Children usually have enormous difficulties. They cannot understand why a parent would
choose to leave them. Are they so unlovable that he
couldn't stay? Was he crazy? Are they crazy? Will
they someday kill themselves? Rather than having a
life of economic ease, most children of suicide victims suffer in dire need.

Ed often flirted with the prospect of ending it all.
He mused over methods. He speculated what death
would feel like. More than once he planned the time
and place. The most important factor that helped
him snap out of these feelings was his children. Ed
read of the effects of suicide on children. He loved
his own two so much that he couldn't let himself
impose the horror on their lives.

One of the reasons why suicide needs to be discussed more and not less is that there are more
myths about it than there are remedies. The potential victim tends to think what he wants. Facts are
often the wedge to bring him to reality.

A psychiatrist tried this bold experiment. He

showed slides to a high-school assembly. They were gruesome pictures he had taken of bodies in an emergency room. Victims of hangings had their blue tongues sticking out. Some had their heads half-blown off.

He kept the students' rapt attention. Many of them had fantasized about suicide. They had considered it a pleasant escape from the pounding problems of life. His presentation helped reestablish the horrors of violent death.

In a gentle but vivid way, the impact of suicide needs to be expressed. No one dies alone. In suicide, the tentacles of pain are particularly long and severe.

Before the two of you part company, be sure to suggest some wholesome alternatives. Part of the reason he is in this situation is his boxed-in feeling. He sees no way out. Name a couple of things that might prove helpful. Possibly there is a job site at which people are being hired. Maybe a trip would be in order. He might need to see a personable marriage counselor. Getting away will be a charm to some but a curse to others. The important factor is a change of pace. He has been hard-pressed and needs to ease up. Any alternative that will relieve the tension can be therapeutic. Your goal is not to solve his problem. The object is to spark hope.

It is also important to suggest you get together again. He needs as many life links as he can collect. Set a definite time and place. If he does not show up, call him. Where distance is a problem, write a letter and ask for a reply. Give him a long-distance call.

Don't assume the crisis is over. Just because the situation has improved does not mean the problem has gone away. Many people commit suicide after a resurgence of strength.

In Oklahoma City, a business executive climbed out on his ninth-floor ledge. The police handled the situation well. They called a friend, who talked on the phone to the distraught businessman. The gentleman obviously calmed down. He came back into his office. After some relaxed talking, he promised the authorities he would seek counseling the first thing in the morning. The police walked him to his car and watched him drive away.

He then drove around a few blocks and returned to his office building. In a matter of minutes he jumped off his ledge.

The individual's problem is not suicide itself, but some deeper trouble. Once the crisis has been averted, we should travel the second mile. Many people can be helped most by our getting them in touch with professional counseling.

Francine Klagsburn calls a counselor "the trained outsider." Possibly it will be a clergyman, a social worker, psychologist, psychiatrist, or other family counselor. The troubled individual needs another person to evaluate his condition and make recommendations. Those who are personally involved with him are often too close to the tension to make an impartial judgment.

Try to reassure the individual that he is not crazy but facing crushing problems. A professional might be able to smooth out the bigger bumps.

It is essential at all times to protect your honesty. Don't promise anything you can't deliver. For instance, it would be foolish to guarantee him that he will only need one visit. Be open and positive. If he sizes you up as a manipulator, you may destroy your effectiveness.

The best way to select a counselor is by choosing someone you already know. That person may not be able to help, but at least he can refer you to someone better equipped. A tuned-in clergyman often has experience and can assist in finding a qualified expert.

Not all psychologists are created equal. Dr. Paul Barkman reminds us that there are as many different thoughts in psychology as there are Protestant denominations. Therefore it may be more reassuring to select a counselor who has been recommended. Someone who has had experience with a particular counselor can give you some idea how he operates.

If there is no one to give a referral, a quick phone call will bring a suggestion. Any of the two hundred suicide prevention centers in the nation will give references.

As time goes by, the individual will need a base of support, more "life links." He may need to meet and become friends with a new group. Often potential suicide victims suffer from critical loneliness.

A local group of accepting Christians can be of immense help. They do not even have to know about the person's problems. All he needs is open arms and steady friendship. It is a mistake, however, to think all Christian groups are this way. Some are extremely judgmental and intolerant. But a positive, outgoing collection of believers can be immensely therapeutic.

In Washington, D.C., an active youth group welcomed David, a man in his early twenties. He showed up one day with an established member of the group and quickly became a part of the fellowship. He was at the socials, played on the ragtag softball team, and eventually gained an office in the department.

One day someone said, "Dave's from St. E's." That was the mental hospital across the Anacostia River. No more than a thimbleful of words. As far as I know, it was all that was ever said about Dave's past. There was no gossip about how he got there. He was just one of us, fully accepted.

Stories similar to this can be multiplied. Christian believers working together as an inclusive community act much like oysters making pearls. A foreign object comes inside, and immediately it is covered over. All its rough edges are smoothed down. After a process of assimilation, it becomes more than it ever thought it could.

The cost of involvement is high. If the person is a relative, you are forced to bear the load. Sometimes you wonder if you can hold up. Others are voluntarily involved. They stick their necks out because they care. In the best spirit of Jesus Christ, they reach their arms out to someone who has trouble standing by himself.

Whatever role we play, the burden is heavy. At

times the person becomes a pest. When the trials are particularly stressful, some will even wish the person would go on and end it. That is a frequent reaction after a deeply involved helper has exhausted his resources. Usually, however, it's a passing feeling, and the helper goes on to be a continuing friend.

There may be no easy way to help a potential suicide, but it is a vital investment in life. Man does few things as noble and nothing more loving.

Eventually someone asks the question "Why don't we leave them alone? If a person wants to kill himself, what business is it of ours?" It's a valid question and deserves a reply.

Briefly, there are two paramount reasons for preventing suicide. The first is the fact that no suicide dies alone. His exodus from life hurts everyone around him. The relatives are crushed the hardest. A high percentage of suicides occur among children whose parents killed themselves. These families and friends will not get over it.

The second reason is that most suicide victims both want to die and want to live. They are crying for help. They are ambivalent and often have trouble thinking clearly. In this state of mind a person is *not* making his own choice. Would we help a stunned man get away from a busy highway? Of course. Then we should extend a hand to stop a potential suicide.

Most people who attempt suicide do not try it again. Given the chance to live, they decide to accept it. We need to give them that chance.

FOURTEEN

AFTER
THE ATTEMPT

"IF WALT REALLY WANTED TO JUMP off that roof, no one could have stopped him. Who does he think he's kidding?"

This statement is entirely true. It's too bad it was said in contempt and not compassion. The fact is that Walt wanted to live, but he also was looking for help. Since he saw no way to get effective assistance, he cried out in the most dramatic way he knew. The vital question now is will he find encouragement, or will he have to take a more drastic step?

We should not imagine Walt standing on top of the building and thinking, "If I stay here for about thirty minutes, everyone will know I have a problem." In all probability, Walt didn't really know what he was going to do. He didn't want to die, and yet he saw no way to live. He was literally in a twilight zone. That is possibly the most crushing dilemma a person will ever face.

Every once in a while an uninformed person will say, "If he wants to kill himself, leave him alone. You can't stop it anyway." The significant fact is that even though a potential suicide wants to die, he also wants to live, but needs someone to show him a way. One man stood on a ledge for eleven hours. Just before leaping, he told a policeman near him, "I only wish someone could convince me that life is worth living."

The first key to restoring an attempter's life is often through his immediate family, even though a large percentage of would-be suicides have lost meaningful communication with their closest relatives. Sometimes, however, the people who can help him the most may hurt him deeply. If a son tries to kill himself, the parents may become immediately hostile. How could he do this to them? They have done so much, and he repays them this way. People will think they have been terrible parents. It is a cruel and thankless thing for a youth to do.

It is perfectly understandable if a parent feels this way. A husband or wife might experience the same thing. Their emotions will be a kaleidoscope of anger, self-pity, bewilderment, and love.

In a sense, an individual is entitled to this array of emotions. They are normal and should be expected. *But our ability to help the attempter is directly related to our ability to conquer our own self-pity.* We love a person who is in tragic difficulty. This is not the time to stop loving him.

Most people who attempt suicide have lost contact with a "significant other." This close personal contact could be a parent, brother, sister, husband, wife, or friend. It is someone the individual felt understood him, someone he could share with.

He may not have actually discussed his most intimate feelings with this "significant other," but he thought he could. He knew that person was there if he needed him and he gained security from that knowledge.

Many who attempt self-destruction have lost such a person, or possibly they never had one. For them, there is no escape valve, and the pressure builds. It is possible to be surrounded by people and to be considered very likable, and still have no one.

If at all possible, it is important to try to become a "significant other," someone who is a sympathetic ear. Not that we have to agree all the time—we lose credibility that way—but we need to be someone who understands, who is patient and kind.

After all the technical jargon about suicide, the matter becomes reduced to simple terms: people's basic needs are for kindness and caring.

The facts of human dynamics tell us not everyone can take on this role of the "significant other." Some may have built too many barriers over the years. For others, the "chemistry" may not be there. For still others, the attempter's personality will not allow it. Sometimes a parent has not been able to in the past, but hopefully he can correct his role in the future.

THE POTENTIAL SUICIDE

But a person who loves and cares has to try. There is the chance that it might work.

It may be that you don't "click" with someone, but a third party does. If so, be ready to accept that. A wife does not have to feel offended if her husband finds good communication with a hunting friend. A parent does not have to feel threatened because his teenager is drawn to a youth director. Be glad he can find someone.

The person who becomes involved in helping an attempter has not selected an easy task. He has to be prepared for a long, unsteady road. Some who have attempted suicide will try again. A few will succeed. But many will recover to lead healthy lives. It is a difficult process, but there is good reason to be optimistic.

In all likelihood the process will take a toll on us. It would be rare to become personally and deeply involved and not pay a price. From the outset, we need to be prepared to sacrifice, but that is generally the price of love.

The attempter always needs people to talk to. He also needs someone during the crisis periods. For most people, thoughts of suicide are not continuous, rather, they come and go. Often the moods are dictated by circumstances, and sometimes there seems to be little rhyme or reason. A close friend needs to be available during these periods.

During the crisis moments, the friend or relative should be prepared to discuss whatever is on the victim's mind. Be careful not to cut him off. If he insists he has committed some terrible sin, don't tell him he hasn't. Ask what it was. Why does he think so? To fight what he is saying only blocks him up. He wants to get something out, and we are telling him, "No, keep it in."

If he wants to discuss suicide in general and his attempt in particular, do not discourage it. To him, the subject is not morbid but realistic. But we also need to help our friend remember there are other topics of conversation as well, some of them bright and beautiful. The close friend will be realistic but optimistic. Sometimes that will be a tough posture to maintain, but the attempter needs as much positive input as possible.

Immediately after the attempt, some vital questions have to be confronted. Will the person need hospitalization? Will he have to be restrained for a while? Is it necessary to call the police?

The first rule of thumb is to do whatever is necessary to save and preserve a life. Where there is life, there is hope. No matter the consequence, save him from destruction.

Then use your best judgment to determine an appropriate referral person. Contact some authority for advice. Whom you ask will depend largely on the circumstances. The police, a physician, a clergyman, a psychologist, or suicide prevention center may be able to help. It is important that you not try to decide what to do on your own. When we are emotionally involved, it is hard to determine what must be done. At that moment, the wise person swallows his pride and responds to the need.

A minister in Maryland was having desperate

trouble with his son. He was determined to counsel the lad himself and "pray him through." The youth only became worse. Finally a court order forced the father to seek outside help. His closeness to the situation limited his potential to cure. It was a large pill for him to take, but it was a necessary one. "Where there is no guidance, a people falls; but in an abundance of counselors there is safety" (Prov. 11:14, RSV).

In our desire to "keep it quiet" we may think we are doing the would-be suicide a favor. In fact, we may be gambling unnecessarily with his life. An attempted suicide is tragic; it would be foolish to call it good. It also seems strange to say, "God had a purpose in this." That response is too simple, and I think, an insult to God. It is true, however, that out of calamity God is able to salvage good. That is the essence of a verse like Romans 8:28. Family and friends now can benefit by asking what good can come from this catastrophe.

One of the lessons we learn is the need to communicate love. Some people who attempt suicide are not convinced they are loved. We need to reevaluate our attitude toward them. In most cases, the problem is not that we don't love them but that we have not communicated our love. Is the individual convinced he is loved? We may even need a counselor ourselves to assess our patterns of communicating love.

Another factor to evaluate might be the area of personal worth. Members of our own family might think too little of themselves because they sense we do not think they are as good as other people. The net effect is a poor self-image. It is not too late to reverse this trend. By acting now, we can have a second chance.

It is also important to practice taking life one day at a time (probably the best way to live under any circumstance). Someone you love has looked death in the face and has been given back to you. There is no way to tell what may happen tomorrow. *Today* we have worked and have had moments to enjoy; *today* we are alive. Thank God for it.

FIFTEEN

THE ROLE
OF THE MINISTER

A BAPTIST MINISTER, Harry Warren, was the first person to open a suicide prevention center in the United States. The year was 1906. At the time, Warren was conducting services in hotels, ministering particularly to the lonely. After his meetings, a number of people would come to him and discuss their intentions to commit suicide.

One day a woman asked a hotel manager to contact a clergyman for her. The manager phoned Warren, but he said he was too busy to come right then. The lady swallowed poison.

When Warren heard of the attempted suicide, he rushed to the hospital. The woman was conscious but dying. She told Warren that if she could have found a clergyman, she would not have tried to kill herself. Then, before she died, she asked him to do everything he could to help people flirting with suicide.

Determined to never repeat this scene again, Warren began an organization to help save the despondent.

Fortunately, millions of hurting people contact a minister first in time of trouble. This leaves the door wide open to help the many who know of no other place to turn.

Ministers know a large number of people, some only superficially, but perhaps they know even their slight acquaintances better than anyone knows them. They have the chance to observe changes in people. They have the opportunity to talk to scores of individuals weekly on a formal and informal basis. Possibly no one is in a better position to help potential suicides and their survivors.

When it comes to suicide prevention, a multiple church staff approach is excellent. If a disturbed person has trouble feeling at home with one minister, he may gravitate toward another. One pastor may have more specific training in an area than the rest of the staff.

McGee and Hiltner in their book *Suicidal Behavior* agree with the strong role played by ministers. In both prevention and aftermath, a clergyman may be in an excellent position to help. The root problems of suicide are often feelings of guilt, worthlessness, and lack of forgiveness. For those who believe in God, these become strong theological issues.

In fact, some problems are intensified by poor theology. The individual may have some gross misconceptions about God and his Word. Possibly they still hold foggy ideas from their childhood or even from recent teachings. In some of these cases, only a minister can adequately move them through the crisis.

Steve was courageously religious. His commitment to Jesus Christ was thorough. He attended meetings, taught classes, witnessed continuously. But despite all his religious activity, he had personal problems that haunted him. He felt plagued by guilt feelings, and he was unable to accept forgiveness. He was convinced the Lord he loved hated him. He also hated himself. Unable to cope with what seemed an impossible struggle, he decided to try to end his life—not because he wanted to do evil, but because of his overwhelming passion to do good.

Years later, regular counselors were still unable to help Steve reconstruct his life. Only a minister whom he respected had a reasonable chance of persuading him that God was not disgusted with him.

The pastorate is undergoing remarkable changes. Many of the new twists are extremely beneficial. Today 20 percent of the nation's clergymen are in parachurch ministries. Some are hospital, prison, and even industrial chaplains. Many are on call at hotels and motels. Some are involved in camp and vacation ministries. Others visit daily on university and high-school campuses. In many ways, the clergy is more accessible to the general public than it has been in the past.

Clergymen have also opened themselves up to broader training. Fifteen years ago, an established pastor argued forcefully with a noted psychiatrist, saying ministers did not need to study counseling. Today, the same pastor has taken several classes and seminars on the subject. Large numbers of clergymen are reading and preparing themselves for a service in personal counseling.

They are also developing an array of referrals. The beginning of maturity is to realize you cannot help everyone. The messiah complex is far less prevalent among ministers than it may have been in the past. Many of the most conservative pastors are now willing to recommend a nearby psychologist if he is needed. For those seeking counseling, a local minister can be a first step.

Jesus Christ offered practical help on family life, jobs, facing enemies, money management. After hearing the Sermon on the Mount, his audience was astonished at Jesus' "doctrine." Many born-again pastors accept practical Christian living as essential to good doctrine.

The pastor who wants to deal with people's needs has to demonstrate interest and understanding from the pulpit. Some parishioners are convinced their minister is concerned only about celestial and mystical matters. People with trouble are more likely to go to someone who believes that the present trials are real.

When a minister goes into the pulpit, he literally has the answers in his hands. The Bible deals with the basic problems behind suicide. Self-destruction is often caused by difficulties common to us all: depression, guilt, lack of self-esteem, loss of hope, envy, hate, self-pity, anxiety. The pastor who deals with these subjects in a biblical, practical manner can help head off many explosions.

One old adage told a pastor to preach with the Bible in one hand and a newspaper in the other. Maybe a sounder recipe is the Bible in one hand and his people's needs in the other.

Most ministers who are interested in counseling people with suicidal thoughts have a number of ways to express their willingness to listen. An occasional mention of the subject in a church bulletin can let people know the minister is open to the topic. Possibly a couple of paragraphs in the monthly church paper will be effective. A sermon dealing directly with the problem may help develop an openness.

Before a pastor approaches the subject, it is essential he get his facts straight. His reading should be of current, reliable material. Theories concerning suicide held fifteen years ago may have been discarded by now. Figures are radically different as records have become more accurate. Trends in self-destruction change with the times. Hopefully, the pastor will not dampen his effectiveness by being misinformed.

Probably the least effective minister is the professional pessimist who preaches endlessly on how hopeless the world is. This is the last thing the potential suicide needs. He is in despair; everything seems rotten. The church appears as a citadel of hope. But instead of finding a healing balm, he listens to the minister describe a dismal, dank world in which no one or nothing can be trusted. The pastor confirms his darkest fears and leaves him more despondent than when he came.

Jesus Christ must be presented as a person of hope. The pastor needs to warn his people of the evil in this world, but he does an injustice if he does not point to the solid solutions Christ offers.

In a large church on the East Coast, a knowledgeable pastor reigned with dignity. Each Sunday he spent forty-five minutes divulging the great mysteries of God. He was erudite, and people bragged about his depth. In some cases, they really meant they couldn't understand him. Most of the congregation would never have approached him with a personal problem. They already knew what to expect: a verse out of Ephesians and an admonition to read the Bible, pray, and have faith. After all, he implied, the stresses in life were really simple matters. Consequently, almost no one went to him.

The real tragedy of the story, however, was that those who were suffering from genuine conflicts were only having their burdens doubled. They read their Bibles and prayed, but their heavy loads did not go away. Since the solution had been tried, they decided something had to be wrong with the patient. The confused, distressed Christian mistakenly thought he was so bad off that God's remedies didn't work on him.

Simplistic answers to complex problems, the waving of a Bible like a magic wand—how many people have been hurt by this approach? Effective pastors believe the Bible contains the answers, but they are willing to work until they find how to apply those solutions to a wounded soul.

Another area in which a pastor can provide help is in ministering to a suicide victim's family. Unless they quickly get good assistance, they could become some of the most severely suffering people in society.

Mrs. Thornton's daughter tried to kill herself. Now she was in counseling and was evidently recovering. But the one who was suffering now was her mother. The girl's counselors had told her to not worry about her attempt. Her condition was really the fault of her parents, especially of her dominating mother, they said. The daughter became hostile and accusing, and her mother was devastated.

This woman was the hidden casualty. She needed someone to help her deal with her feelings. A wise pastor will seek her out and give her the open door for counseling.

As we mentioned earlier, surviving children will also suffer from deep wounds. Pastors can go a long way toward resolving their fears and some of their nightmares.

Each member of the family needs plenty of opportunity to talk, to voice apprehensions, questions, doubts. The pastor becomes a listening board, but he is also a doctor. He can recommend solutions and guidelines. He can share the broad, comforting smile of God to begin rebuilding some shattered lives.

PART FOUR

WHERE TO GO FROM HERE

SIXTEEN

HOW DO
I HANDLE
MY FEELINGS?

WHEN SUICIDE HAS TOUCHED YOUR LIFE, you can expect to feel practically every shade of emotion. Anger, guilt, love, denial, compassion, self-pity, and confusion are just starters. Your heart will soon seem wrung dry. At times you will wish you could not feel anything.

None of us should be surprised at the depth of the wound. Three years after a suicide, most survivors still cannot bring themselves even to discuss the subject. The emotional impact on family and friends is generally greater than any other form of death.

But this endless suffering is not necessary. Some survivors recover to lead healthy, energetic lives. Many more could recover if they were able to express and handle their honest emotions.

The first reaction of most survivors is denial. They not only resist the fact of death, but even more intensely they reject the method. But when the material evidence and the psychological history are irrefutable, only harm can come from denying the facts.

The survivor must be honest with himself. He cannot afford to spend years playing Ping-Pong with his own feelings.

Some people will never know what caused their relative's death. They should be encouraged to think positively. But for others, the facts are incontrovertible. The healthiest thing they can do is admit the death was a suicide and start to rebuild their own lives.

A mother in Spokane tried desperately to hide her feelings from her daughter. She told the young child that her father had died from a heart attack. Naturally, the girl believed her. The daughter grew up, however, with a strange dislike for her father and for all men. Even though the mother had refused to communicate the fact of suicide, she had unknowingly carried a hostility toward her dead husband. That feeling was transmitted and assimilated by the girl. The young lady did not know why she did not like her dad, but she knew the negative feelings were there.

Hidden, smothered feelings can be terribly dangerous, and wearing our emotions on our sleeve can be equally detrimental. A healthy expression at the correct time is medicine to a sagging heart.

The first and most important step is to ask yourself how you really feel. Do you hate the person who died or attempted suicide? Then be honest with yourself. If so, do you *want* to hate him? Will you continue to hate him? What will happen if you continue?

To merely say, "I know how I feel," is not enough. After identifying your emotions, you want to ask what to do next. Are there conflicts that need to be resolved? Can you find some help in working out those feelings? For some, guilt will hang like wet fog. Be specific. Why do you feel that way? Is there factual basis for it? What should you do now?

Most people find the best way to work through their emotions is to talk them out with a trustworthy individual. When they explain their feelings, it helps them define what is going on. It helps them release the pressure. Often while talking, they come up with their own solution.

If possible, talk freely with your closest relatives and friends. The best policy is honesty without trying to shock everyone.

Another channel for many is to talk openly to God. He doesn't shock easily, and he's terrific at keeping secrets. When we sit still and meditate, he may even help resolve some feelings. Communication with God is important, but he *refuses* to be the only source. He surrounded most of us with people, and he anticipates we will use them for our own good.

"For he has not despised my cries of deep despair; he has not turned and walked away. When I cried to him, he heard and came" (Ps. 22:24).

As the survivors sift out their feelings, they will try to understand why their loved one took his own life. What kind of pressures did he face, internally and externally? How long did he agonize?

There is no doubt he hurt those he left. But in the process of recovery, it will be helpful to remember his serious trials. His suffering was acute. He felt his mind viciously torn between life and death.

It is also important to know that if he could, he would have remained with his family. This will be a hard fact to accept, but in most cases it is true. The victim did not want to die. He wanted to stay, to love and be loved. Statistics bear this out in almost every case. He battled back and forth and then gave in. This does not justify what he did. But possibly it helps explain the confused bowl of feelings he was trying to sort out. He rejected the people he loved, but in most cases, he loved the people he rejected. He felt he couldn't leave, and yet he couldn't stay. Finally, confusion took its dreadful toll.

The easiest thing for survivors to do is jump on the slide of self-pity. It is smooth and slick, but it always travels down. Self-pity has never picked anyone up. How survivors handle this critical attitude may determine their emotional health for the rest of their lives.

Self-pity has an ugly pattern. When left unchecked, it follows a predictable course—degenerating into anger, then bitterness, then depression. In extreme cases, it explodes into violence.

Realizing the crippling agony of self-pity, the wise

person will step up to life. He tells himself, "I have decided to live." He will then aim his goals at rebuilding and creating a future he can find fulfilling.

To a large extent, we can aim our minds in whatever direction we choose. The Bible tells us to point toward hopeful, positive, wholesome goals. "Finally, brothers, whatever is true, whatever is noble, whatever is right, whatever is pure, whatever is lovely, whatever is admirable—if anything is excellent or praiseworthy—think about such things" (Phil. 4:8).

A significant way to resolve our feelings is to gather information on the subject. Ignorance about suicide permeates our society. The more people are educated, the less mystical horror will hover over the word. Every family touched by suicide will want to collect some reliable literature and learn about the subject—and about themselves.

Warnings need to be given on this type of literature. A preoccupation with suicide can be injurious to your health. Some survivors bury themselves in information and make suicide the center of their lives. They mull over the topic endlessly until it becomes an obsession.

A healthy life can be regained by broadening interests and vowing to live again. Read about the subject only until you are informed; then lay it aside and determine not to dwell on it.

One way to escape self-pity and introspection is to concentrate on helping the others involved. Children, parents, brothers, and close friends are all grieving to some degree, possibly for different reasons. If we can take our eyes off our own loss, these people could benefit from our attention.

It is hard to know how much should be discussed with whom. A particular group to be aware of are close friends of the victim, especially a youth's boyfriend or girl friend. These individuals have made themselves vulnerable by being personally involved with a human being. Their friend has decided to end his life. This is usually a terrible blow to a companion, who is often ignored in the healing process.

A busy college student named Erich had long talks with his roommate Gary. Gary was deeply disturbed and seemingly had endless problems. One spring day, he threw himself out the dormitory window.

Erich's grief was crippling. He felt definitely at fault. If he had been a better friend, he reasoned, Gary would still be alive. Erich needed extensive counseling before he could continue his college career.

Some comforting words from the immediate family could have benefited Erich greatly—reassurance that they did not hold him responsible, possibly information that Gary had problems before he met Erich. There would have been no need for an elaborate dissertation. Love and tenderness would probably have been as helpful as anything.

It is hard to know how much to share with friends and relatives. Each person will probably need to use his own personal gauge. Certainly you owe nothing to the crude and curious. They can be terribly rude.

Like vultures soaring around, each rumor becomes a tantalizing morsel for them. Be polite, but do not feel obligated to feed their appetites.

Closer friends are another matter. What does the person mean to you, and how much have you shared in the past? To a few you will want to tell everything. They want to help by listening, and you need a compassionate ear. The more you can discuss freely, the better.

If your family member has survived an attempted suicide, the entire matter takes on a different dimension. Your loved one's integrity has to be protected. Find help for yourself, but don't hurt the attempter in the process.

A college student from a small town tried to end his life by an overdose. He spent two weeks under mental observation and was released. The day he came home, his family firmly assured him his school friends had not been told. The lad found it easier to mix freely, because he felt certain no one knew. The attempter is entitled to this promise whenever feasible.

The stigma around suicide is still enormous. Those who are told the full story need to be carefully selected.

SEVENTEEN

WHAT ABOUT
THE CHILDREN?

"WHAT DID I DO that made my mother kill herself?"

It is hard to imagine a sadder sentence in the English language. But this is what thousands of children are asking themselves every year. They may ask it for the rest of their lives. Perhaps no survivors suffer greater than the children who are left bewildered.

For many decades suicide was thought to be hereditary. The logic appeared to be sound. If a high number of children of suicides later select self-destruction themselves, there must be a biological explanation. In 1909 Newton Riddell quoted Griesinger, "Experience has shown that the inclination to suicide, which often comes on in all members of a family at the same age, communicates itself by hereditary descent." The author then goes on to illustrate his point by a man who hanged himself. Three of his four sons in turn committed suicide.

Today we know better. It is true there is a high percentage of suicides among children of suicides. But there are no evidences that biological heredity has anything to do with it.

The surviving child is usually left in a terribly confused state of mind. He does not understand exactly what has happened and certainly not why. In most cases, he is smothered by feelings of guilt, anger, and insecurity. If these emotions are not handled successfully, the youth may suffer dire consequences.

Dr. Shneidman has worked extensively with suicides and their families. He now emphasizes what is called "postvention," the healing of lives damaged by the suicide of a close relative or friend.

When left to themselves, survivors pay a terribly high price for suicide. As Dr. Shneidman points out, individuals who commit suicide very often sentence the survivors to be obsessed for the rest of their lives about the suicidal death.

Kurt Vonnegut, Jr., has said, "Sons of suicides seldom do well." But if a child of a suicide victim receives the right type of help at the correct time, his prospects can be improved dramatically.

The first question that arises is whether or not to tell the children. In most families, the reaction to suicide is twofold. The survivors attempt to deny the facts even to themselves, no matter what the physical evidence and previous threats indicate. This is perfectly understandable. Suicide is a devastating experience.

The second reaction is to cover it up. In many areas the police, doctors, and newspapers will help. If there is the slightest doubt, they might, out of kindness, rule against suicide as the cause. As one person put it, "It's nobody's business if someone killed himself." There is some merit to this argument.

When it comes to the family and friends, however, the attitude of concealment becomes dangerous. Suppose the child is not told by the people who love him or her. What are some of the other possibilities?

The child might guess it was suicide. The young person notices all the whispering. Maybe when people mention the cause of death they don't look the child in the eye or else they start to cry. Possibly the child cannot justify the odd behavior of the parent before he died. Maybe he wasn't sick but passed suddenly. Some things do not jell in the youth's mind.

It would be erroneous to think children are easily pacified about death. A five year old often has a sharp interest in the subject, and trying to shut off his mind does not mean it has closed down.

Will the child find out the truth by innuendo? A neighbor might try to find out if the child knows what happened. Leading questions start the imagination. Some of his playmates may even say some cruel things he is not prepared to handle.

The first advantage to leveling with the child is being able to control the circumstances. The family can make sure the information is correct and is said in a loving, compassionate way. Time can be devoted to answering questions, hugging, and even crying.

When the situation is stifled, fears go unresolved. The scars will be deep. There may be no healthy therapeutic release.

For Christian children these problems may be more intense. Has God condemned their mother? Was she even a Christian? Why did not God stop it? These are serious questions that should be encouraged rather than choked off.

Once the decision has been made to be frank but gentle, a second hurdle has to be confronted. Will anything be said at the funeral about the method of death? Since most people in attendance are thinking about it anyway, some reference may be helpful. If the clergyman simply ignores the fact, it may add to the feeling of shame. A reference to suicide could help reduce the tension and assure everyone that a medieval attitude is not prevailing.

The child can add up the facts. Mother has ended her own life. Dad still loves her. Our friends don't condemn her. The minister seems to be understanding. Maybe mother was not a bad person after all.

Dr. Shneidman and other authorities recommend a visit between the children and a counselor soon after the death. The counselor may be a psychologist, psychiatrist, school counselor, or clergyman. But they need a sympathetic, authoritative, compassionate figure to talk with.

Parents are often not enough, though they are of paramount importance. In a sense, the child will benefit from a second opinion. He needs to be reassured his surviving parent is not simply trying to make him feel good.

The child may also need someone to listen, maybe even to pry a little. No person can always guess what another person, child or adult, is thinking. One young boy might believe the mother killed herself because he refused to go to the store for her, or he may wonder if he nagged too much about a new bike.

Some children will want to know whether the parent was crazy. They may also wonder if they themselves are mentally ill. Possibly they will believe a curse is following them that they cannot escape.

The only way to fathom some of these thoughts is to answer pertinent questions honestly and allow plenty of time for talking.

Naturally, some will object to so much emphasis and attention on the death. They will feel that the less said the better and that everyone should try to forget it. Studies show this to be the least effective and usually the most damaging approach. Survivors need to release their feelings, and resolve their questions, not internalize their troubles.

The age and maturity of the child play important factors in the discussion. How much they are told often depends on their questions and grasp of the situation. There should be no attempt to fool the child, but there needs to be care not to overwhelm him with information he can't comprehend.

The key to healthy recovery for children is usually the surviving parent. If he is making good strides to recovery, the child has a much better chance. The survivor who fails to cope with reality will only add to the youth's wounds.

Attitudes toward the deceased parent are extremely important. If the survivors show hostility toward the victim, the children will think they should. The wise parent will try to give the child some wholesome concepts and memories to hold on to. The adults close to the situation need to exercise presence of mind so that the child's needs may be met as quickly as possible. Those first impressions are all important.

Anniversaries of the suicide are also hard days. Some children have nightmares and periods of despondency. Authorities on the subject recommend the family receive special love during this period. Possibly they can get together with friends or somehow find a way to escape the full brunt of the occasion.

Deep feelings of guilt are also found among those whose brother or sister has committed suicide. Often they recall mean things they said or did to the deceased. They can even remember times when they "wished the pest were dead." These memories now haunt them, and they are extremely hard on themselves.

These intense emotions are more widespread than is popularly believed. If a fifteen-year-old boy kills himself and leaves two younger brothers, they will have great difficulties. How did they contribute to this horror? Will they do the same thing? These children need attention as soon as possible.

Francine Klagsburn tells of a college student who sucked his thumb. He was four years old when his father committed suicide. The youth lives in constant fear and insecurity.

With the correct assistance, many children are able to gain a balanced life. But if a healthy memory of the deceased parent is to be restored, there must be careful, considerate work deliberately done by someone who cares. Many of us come in contact with the children of suicides and never know it. They are businessmen, entertainers, housewives, and government officials. They are living evidence that there is hope after a serious blow.

EIGHTEEN

DO I NEED PROFESSIONAL HELP?

IN THE PROCESS OF LOOKING OUT for everyone else, we are likely to forget ourselves. There is something therapeutic about being able to concentrate on others, but it can be dangerous to ignore the problems building inside.

If someone close to you has committed suicide or attempted it, you have problems. It would be unwise to ignore those difficulties or try to smother them. They are lurking around in the back of your consciousness, and they insist on being answered sooner or later.

How will the suicide affect your life? Will it haunt you in the future? Are you in some way responsible? Is suicide contagious and likely to affect you?

WHERE TO GO FROM HERE

The person who decided to end his life was part of a chain. His life and death have consequences for everyone else in his family or close circle. Some of those will ride out the storm well. Most will not if they don't allow someone to help them.

Say to yourself emphatically, "I have a problem." Admit it face on. Then say, "I am going to do something about it." You owe it to yourself, to your family, and to everyone around you.

In many cases of extreme distress such as suicide, the entire family is automatically involved. Certain tensions in the home may have contributed heavily to the emergency. The family may have no positive form of communication. There may exist an inbred feeling of inferiority. It possibly permeates from generation to generation. This personality assassination needs to end. Hopefully, an outside counselor can assist in restoring self-esteem.

It may be that love is genuine in the home and yet the children are not aware of it. Other family members might be about to burst open with frustration because there is no conventional way to release it. In some homes the emotional lid is screwed on so tightly that an explosion is inevitable.

If the situation is to improve, the entire family may need group and personal counseling. Those in a position to make decisions need to seriously consider possible solutions. Those in the middle of a situation are often the least able to evaluate the problems.

If you will lead the way in seeking and accepting help, the rest of the family may be greatly benefited.

In some areas, family therapists are available. They come into the home and meet with everyone. Their job is to weigh all the dynamics and relationships and make suggestions for improvements. This course of action may be needed whether the individual has attempted or completed the suicide. Either way the problems are drastic.

Most of us feel it is important to put on a front. This isn't all bad. The ideal is not to wear all our emotions on our sleeve, but taken to the extreme, stonewalling can have detrimental consequences. It is far better to confront our problems rather than let them consume us.

Whatever position you hold in the family, the threat of suicide has its peculiar pains. A surviving child has his set of troubles to face. A parent is shackled with an assortment of conflicts. A married spouse has yet another list of difficulties.

Someone with a stable background may have married a disturbed individual, hoping that marriage and someone who cares is all that person needs for stability. Once in a while this does work out, but more likely the problem remains; insecurities are often deep and not easily resolved.

When a mate is in distress, there is no more powerful hold than the threat of suicide. It is literally a death lock. The partner does not know how to respond. Should she call his bluff and tell him to go ahead? Is the best step to simply move out until he "grows up"?

Any direction she chooses she may regret all her life. She will wonder if she was the cause for his intense despair. This person needs help! She needs it immediately. The couple is skating on the thin ice of continuous anxiety. Not only might her husband do something irreversible, but so could she. An individual normally can survive only so long under pressure.

A man in Oregon often threatened to kill himself. His wife wavered over whether it was best to stay or leave. Every time their conflicts raged he resumed his warnings. Finally the husband turned a shotgun on himself. He didn't die, but his wounds were crippling. She was overwhelmed with guilt by his desperate action. Today she has to feed and care for him. He has acquired the pampering he always wanted. By waiting on him, she tries to relieve the load of guilt she feels. Both needed professional help.

The psalm writer wrestled with the same questions we do. How long do we hold it in and try to be brave? "I said to myself, I'm going to quit complaining! I'll keep quiet, especially when the ungodly are around me. But as I stood there silently the turmoil within me grew to the bursting point. The more I mused the hotter the fires inside. Then at last I spoke, and pled with God" (Ps. 39:1-3).

Silence is usually more harmful than constructive. The person who tries to hide his feelings isn't very successful in the long run. Communication is inevitable. For example, the remaining parent decides she will smother her real emotions. She actually resents the person who attempted suicide but has decided to cover it up. Research indicates the children know how their mother feels, even if she says nothing, by the looks on her face, her subtle comments, and even her voice inflection. We forget how well our children know us. The attempt to stifle ourselves is injurious to both the youngsters and ourselves.

Part of the reason we would rather not talk about it is because we are not sure how we feel. Our mood fluctuates from contempt to compassion. Which best describes our real emotions? How do we differentiate between how we feel and how we think we should feel? Emotions are like a moving tide that comes in and out. Add to this our sense of guilt. Sometimes we don't want to let anyone know what we are thinking because we are ashamed of it.

If we can find someone to listen, it may help us sift our thoughts and evaluate them. In order to do this effectively, it would be wise to find an experienced, trained ear. The process may not take long, but certainly some things need to be aired out. The sooner they are vented, the better for everyone.

Who you choose to talk with may depend on your circumstances and location, but find one of the following in your own community:

• Clergymen can help you. We have discussed them elsewhere in the book. Many have good training, considerable experience, and sincere compassion. Since many problems surrounding suicide are theological in nature, a minister may be of unique, specialized service.

If for some reason you would prefer another minister, be open enough to ask for a referral.

WHERE TO GO FROM HERE

Maybe you know your clergyman too well. Possibly you would feel freer with an outsider. By all means ask your minister to set up an appointment with another clergyman. Tell him briefly why, and he will understand. Sometimes this will be far more productive than using your local minister.

• Counseling and diagnostic psychologists are well-trained professionals in the field. Their approach deals more with counseling than testing or medicine. They may rely less on the individual's past and concentrate on his present and future.

• Another route you may choose is to see a clinical psychologist. These are college graduates with extensive postgraduate work in psychology. They are capable of diagnosing, testing, and most of all, listening well. Many have excellent track records for helping. The best way to select one is on the recommendation of a pleased client or another professional. Most large colleges and universities have one or more clinical psychologists on their staff.

• Psychiatrists are often excellent sources of help. They are medical doctors who have specialized in mental illness. Often they are more difficult to find. Psychiatrists are the only members of the mental health team who can prescribe drugs and other medication.

• Psychoanalysts are usually psychiatrists who have had even more specialized training. They usually work with patients as individuals or in groups over a long period of time.

• Psychiatric social workers are college graduates with special training in social work. Their background stresses study in mental health problems within the context of the family. They are especially capable of working with patients and their families who have had initial contacts with a psychologist or psychiatrist.

Most people who need help will not go after it. They have decided to suffer instead. If your relative has committed suicide or has attempted it, you need help. You may need only one or two sessions, or possibly several. But the best chance of reconstructing a solid life is by beginning with some trained, understanding help.

NINETEEN

REBUILDING
MY LIFE

Your life has been seriously wounded by suicide. Nothing can change that fact. You won't wake up tomorrow and discover you were dreaming. There is no philosophical argument that will recolor your experience.

But fortunately, there is today and the opportunity to live again. And that is the decision you have made: you choose to live. Not because it is easy to go on; life does hold its agonies. Some days it is like a salmon attacking the onrushing stream. There will be a large share of knocks and setbacks. It would be easy to sink into self-pity. There is the temptation to lick your wounds and feel sorry for yourself. After all, life has been hard. The ghost of suicide wants to haunt you every day and spread your misery as far as it can. Maybe you will just let it.

Do that. Do it for a week or two. To be perfectly honest, there is genuine comfort in feeling pity. It's almost like hugging yourself to chase the blues away. But don't rock too long. It quickly becomes a habit that might destroy the rest of your life.

Then tell yourself once again that you have chosen to live. You will not have a daily death of regrets. Rather, you will live a life as fulfilling as you possibly can. Congratulations!

Whatever role you played—the attempter, the relative, or the friend—the message is the same: you will live again—because you want to. But in order for that life to be full, it is necessary to take certain courageous steps.

After deciding to abandon self-pity, an individual takes a pledge to not "hole up." It would be simple to withdraw from society and cut everyone off, feeling our life is a private affair that would be smoother if everyone left us alone. In the long run, however, isolation will only hurt most of us. We tend to become paranoid. Our imagination conjures up fabled conversations. We are sure people are wagging their tongues and spreading rumors. The best way to combat these fears is to get out among the community. The facts are almost never as severe as we think.

No matter what others know about us or say, the best remedy for heartache is a happy life. Lift your head high, hold out your chest, and step into the crowd. You understand what has really happened in your life; your genuine friends will also understand; the rest don't count.

Some people may talk about you. They do it for a variety of reasons. A few are terminally vicious. They enjoy nothing more than to smear others. Let this crew go. They are impossible to extinguish and are not worth the effort of fighting. The Bible tells us something about praying for them. But if you decide to resent everybody, your life can only become bitter. You are better off to concentrate on the kind and loving friends.

Since you have decided to live your own life, some significant questions are in order. For instance, how long do you have left? Take a pencil and paper and try some basic arithmetic. Assume you are going to live to be ninety-five. After all, you might! If you are sixty-five, you may have only thirty years to go. Those forty-five may be restricted to a remaining fifty. At twenty-five, there could be a resounding seventy years ahead of you. Draw out a plan of how you would like to spend the decades to come.

Some people can mark the date of their death. They stopped living in August, 1970. That is when their husband died. Since then, they have sustained themselves, eaten, slept, and managed to keep going. They are the walking dead. Someday the facts of nature will claim their bodies, but death has long since occurred. They failed to rebuild their lives.

People will read this book whose lives ceased long ago. It ended the day suicide touched them. A person whom they loved may have chosen self-destruction. When the loved one died, their life ended. For others, it was when their relative attempted suicide. They have not gotten over the shock and do not plan to. A third group gave up living when they themselves tried to end their own lives. Now they are convinced they are crazy. The rest of their days are spent trying to finish the race even if it is only walking to the finish line.

But others have picked up their heads and planned on living. In essence they say, "If I am going to live to be ninety-five, I might as well make the most of it." They have vowed not to join the walking dead. They will rebuild their lives.

For some, the decision to live means going back to school. In the past, they wanted to be a lawyer, an engineer, or an auto mechanic. It may take two years or six to gain that skill, but why not? Some of us may have fifty to sixty years left. A friend of mine farmed for six years in order to save enough money to attend medical school. Today he is a respected physician in our town.

Maybe this route means going to secretarial school, earning a teacher's certificate, or obtaining vocational training. Whatever it is—a positive, strong, self-fulfilling step—you will need courage to carry through, but that accomplishment may be just what you need for a new start.

A woman in the Chicago area was faced with this exact situation. Her husband evidently committed suicide. She was never quite certain. She had two small children and a lifetime to go. Immediately she resolved to not become a perpetual mourner. One year later she enrolled in college to complete her training. In a short time, this courageous lady was teaching and supporting her family. She voted for life.

For others, the future does not include training; it calls for reentry into the job market. But whatever the choice, the goal must be the same: positive, constructive action.

Readers will protest that their situation is different. They have grown overweight. They have no nice clothes. They are afraid to meet people. They have no skills. Each one is a real problem. But each obstacle can be overcome by the person who is determined to live rather than languish.

"But I'm fifty years old." That only gives you forty-five years to go.

Work in itself is not the total spark of life. Personal accomplishments outside the job can add considerable strength. Usually they take initiative and desire.

A lady in California has decided to fight walking death by becoming involved in extra activities. She bowls once a week (though not well) and has joined a civic club. It takes some sacrifice on her part to get out and get going, but she is flintlike. She refuses to stay home and rust. Last December, this sparkling lady played Santa Claus in a department store. Everyone thought she was a he. When she took a tot up on her lap, her "Ho! Ho!" just rolled and her eyes glistened. Her jolly manner said, "I'm going to stay alive the rest of my life."

Fraternal groups, church organizations, hobby clubs, and musical assortments are waiting for people—especially for those who want to give life a good whack. Ask around and gather information about which outlet might best suit your situation.

All of us are dreamers. Every Sunday we look through the travel section of the newspaper. Those beautiful Bavarian Alps with their snowcapped peaks. Deep-sea fishing in the Gulf of Mexico. Gliding across the hills of Southern California. Then we fold up the paper, lay down on the couch, and take a nap. We go places only in our dreams.

The same thing could happen in rebuilding our lives. We would like to put ourselves together, but we cannot seem to get along. Discouraged, we roll back into our misery. We have decided to become professional mourners.

But not everybody. Certainly not you. Right now, stand up, open your arms and smile. Then say out loud, "I have decided to live!"

TWENTY

THERE IS HOPE
FOR TOMORROW

WHY DOES ANYONE WANT TO DISCUSS a morbid
subject like suicide? Do we get a kick from staring
tragic death in the eye? There is only one valid
reason to read this book or study the topic. The facts
prove there is hope for those caught in this mashing
machine.

Every study affirms that most people think about
suicide sometime. Most people, however, do not kill
themselves. There are healthy alternatives and millions of people are finding them.

Many who used to be suicidal are so no longer.
Thousands who have been rocked by a close suicide
have been able to stabilize and construct happy lives.

One source of outstanding strength for many has
been the Bible. It gives a balanced view of man: We

are sinners and we are saints. We are good and bad. We are weak and strong. The Bible understands us and is ready to offer help.

A major factor in suicide is often a feeling of intense inferiority. The victim thinks he can't do anything right. He isn't as good as other people, and he doubts his ability in every situation.

God teaches us to have a positive attitude toward ourselves. Jesus Christ stated the principle crisply, "Love your neighbor as yourself" (Matt. 22:39). He fully expected man to love himself—that is not a sin. Selfishness is wrong, but not self-respect. There is no merit to starving to death so we can feed others. Rather, we take care of ourselves so we will be healthy enough to extend our strength.

The famous musician Roger Williams says he has two signs over his piano. One says, "All love begins with self-love." The second reads, "All respect begins with self-respect."

Our society is cursed with two excesses. The first is self-love with no concern for others. The second is self-hatred. The Bible paints both as being deadly.

It is possible to love and hate yourself at the same time; they are not exclusive feelings. The person who killed himself may have wanted to do himself a favor. He could not stand living, so he decided to relieve his conflicts by ending his life. In the same sense, someone can have an inferiority and superiority complex at the same time.

What some people need is the assurance that it is all right to love themselves. We all need to remember to dress well, exercise, eat the right foods, and take a vacation now and then. It is good to express your love for yourself. But at the same time, we need to remember not to overdo it until we become merely self-centered.

Some psychologists believe there is a definite increase in self-defacing. More of us are unhappy with ourselves. The result is a higher number of suicides due to internal pressure. A person can have everything going for him and still be miserable. He simply does not like himself.

An individual can survive two divorces, a bankrupt business, and loss of friends and be barely moved. Inside he believes he is cool and undaunted by setbacks. He may be unrealistic, but he is pleased with himself. He will endure while the sensitive person will struggle.

The Bible tells us, "Do not think of yourself more highly than you ought" (Rom. 12:3). But then it tells us in the same passage to think highly of ourselves. Paul lists the many gifts we have. God created us to be talented, valuable people. The better we can accept this fact, the more balanced life we can have.

Closely linked to intense inferiority is the plague of personal guilt. People feel guilty, sometimes without knowing why. This feeling can be called "ghost guilt." Their hearts are haunted and they cannot get hold of it.

The Scripture can help; part of its job is to identify and clear up guilt. The Bible meets us where we are. If we have done anything wrong, the Bible will verify it and tell us what to do. However, if we are innocent, we can be reassured.

There are a few simple steps to handling guilt. First of all, identify the fact. Did you do something wrong? Haunting, floating guilt is devastating. Most of us have fouled up someplace recently. It is important to pinpoint the problem and deal with it.

If you cannot decide if you were wrong, there are several ways to find out. Check the Bible, ask a respected person for advice, talk it over with God. "Through the law we become conscious of sin" (Rom. 3:20). When we can't pinpoint a sin, we should leave the past with God and forget it. There is no sense in being dogged by false guilt.

If we can identify a sin, we need to confess it so the guilt can be wiped away. Possibly we need to apologize to God, or maybe to another person. Either way, we remove the weight of guilt by admitting our fault. From that point we are free. God does not hold anything against us. We can go on with a life aimed at tomorrow. "If we confess our sins, he is faithful and just and will forgive us our sins and purify us from all unrighteousness" (1 John 1:9).

The Bible is a double-strength friend. When we are wrong, it tells us what to do about it; when we are innocent, it reminds us we are free.

Hostility is another leading factor among suicide victims. The person who attempts to end his life is often angry at other people and himself. Dr. Karl Menninger wrote years ago that every suicide is a form of misplaced aggression.

Relatives and friends of the suicide victim also display a high degree of anger. They are often hostile toward the person who did the act. How could he be so cruel and inconsiderate as to do this to them?

Jesus knew there were some valid times to get angry. On more than one occasion, he showed people just how upset he was. He let it out when the situation called for it.

Most of the time, however, he refused to get rattled. Anger was a dangerous emotion, and he dispensed it sparingly. Jesus shocked his audience by saying, "You have heard that it was said, 'Love your neighbor and hate your enemy.' But I tell you, Love your enemies" (Matt. 5:44).

Christ attempted to diffuse most tension by exercising love. What good does it do to hate? It only erodes both the hater and the hated. Left unchecked, the feelings can erupt into pain, agony, and sometimes self-destruction. Relentless hostility can be in itself self-destroying.

At times people have handled the Scripture poorly. Instead of doing their appointed job of lifting people up, some teachers have only succeeded in putting them down. But we have a positive model in the apostle John, who clearly declared his wholesome intentions: "Dear friend, I pray that you may enjoy good health and that all may go well with you, even as your soul is getting along well" (3 John 2).

The word *hope* appears 140 times in the Bible and the concept shows up even more often. Constructive, positive, upbeat is the message of Scripture.

The New Testament is packed with guidance in developing wholesome families in which the best possible attitudes of love and security exist. It contains instruction to help parents enable their children to think well of their abilities and worth. Some children will grow up having serious conflicts no matter what type of home they come from. Environment is not the sole determining factor. In more than one home, the parents have done their conscientious best, and yet the child does not make it. Ultimate decisions do rest with the individual. But parents can help their children by establishing well-defined boundaries and liberties. Troubled families more often produce troubled people. Frequently, a shaky family has cut itself off from healthy, outgoing activities, and communication within the home has become a chilly or gruff silence.

Drastic changes in a family can result in damaging circumstances. Young people as well as adults have trouble coping with radical disruptions. One child out of six is presently being raised by one parent. With a greater number of homes being split, more tragedies may be the result.

The Bible can furnish structure to our families by providing authority and a definition of roles. Great latitude exists within this structure, but the necessary boundaries are presented.

Christ also helps us take our eyes off ourselves. Few human dynamics are more destructive than self-pity. The New Testament encourages us to become involved in the needs of other people. Doing things for other people builds our self-confidence and worth. When we are accomplishing something, we are taking a significant step toward breaking our moodiness and inactivity. Looking outward also helps us to see the problems others are facing. When we get that perspective, our irritations fade into nothing.

Paul put it this way, "Each of you should look not only to your own interests, but also to the interest of others" (Phil. 2:4).

A certain amount of introspection is cleansing and essential to growth. Unfortunately some Christians become buried under themselves. Too much self-inspection is crippling. Those involved in the complexity of suicide can find release by becoming concerned about the needs of others.

Another major block that God is anxious to alleviate is the pressure of loneliness. He realizes that most people, left to themselves, will race downhill. They lose faith, they fail to love, their concepts of life often become unfocused. Boredom and discontent are terrible drugs dulling a person's outlook on life.

Creative brooding can lead to constructive action. But sulking is destructive.

Among the middle-aged and elderly who attempt suicide, one condition is predominant: isolation. People need people, and God tells us to get together: "Let us hold unswervingly to the hope we profess, for he who promised is faithful. And let us consider how we may spur one another on toward love and good deeds. Let us not give up meeting together, as some are in the habit of doing, but let us encourage one another—and all the more as you see the Day approaching" (Heb. 10:23-25).

For many it is painful to associate with others. They may feel they have nothing to offer and people will not like them. Out of consideration for our own mental health, we need to seek out and find friends, with whom we can talk and feel comfortable. They may not need to know our deepest emotions in order to serve as a healthy outlet for us.

Every year, thousands find meaning by placing their faith in Jesus Christ. He becomes an important other person who cares, who listens. Then that individual finds he is able to believe in a person outside himself.

Christ offers a set of standards to live by, a firm footing to stand on, something dependable in life. Those who trust their lives to Christ still have struggles, but they also have hope. Christ would like to wrestle some of these problems with us. There are many pictures in the New Testament of the hope Christ can give all of us.

> The jailer woke up, and when he saw the prison doors open, he drew his sword and was about to kill himself because he thought the prisoners had escaped. But Paul shouted, "Don't harm yourself! We are all here!"
>
> The jailer called for lights, rushed in and fell trembling before Paul and Silas. He then brought them out and asked, "Men, what must I do to be saved?"
>
> They replied, "Believe in the Lord Jesus, and you will be saved—you and your household." (*Acts 16:27-31*)

WHERE TO GO FROM HERE

Two things happened quickly to change the jailer's life. First, immediate steps were taken to prevent the suicide. Paul reasoned with him concerning the circumstances. They were not as bad as he had first thought. He could go on living, and things could work out.

Second, the counselor offered him a meaning to life. Paul introduced him to Jesus Christ. There was hope for tomorrow, because Christ was alive.

These basic two ingredients are still essential in suicide prevention. The act itself has to be averted by whatever means necessary. Then the individual has to be offered a reason to live, given some prospect that tomorrow could be different. Jesus Christ gives that living hope.

HELPFUL READING

Alvarez, A. **The Savage God.** New York: *Random House,* 1972.

Choron, Jacques. **Suicide.** New York: *Charles Scribners Sons,* 1972.

Farber, Maurice L. **The Theory of Suicide.** New York: *Funk and Wagnalls,* 1968.

Grollman, Earl A. **Suicide Prevention, Intervention, Postvention.** Boston: *Beacon Press,* 1971.

Klagsburn, Francine. **Too Young to Die.** Boston: *Houghton Mifflin Company,* 1976.

Kohl, Marvin (ed.). **Beneficial Euthanasia.** Buffalo: *Prometheus Books,* 1975.

Parker, A. Morgan, Jr. **Suicide Among Young Adults.** New York: *Exposition Press,* 1974.

Resnik, H. L. P. (ed.). **Suicidal Behaviors.** Boston: *Little, Brown and Company,* 1968.

Shneidman, Edwin S. **The Psychology of Suicide.** *Science House,* 1970.

Shneidman, Edwin S. (ed.). **On the Nature of Suicide.** San Francisco: *Jossey-Bass, Inc.,* 1969.

Stengel, Edwin. **Suicide and Attempted Suicide.** New York: *Penguin Books,* 1973.

Pamphlets

Frederick, Calvin J. "Dealing with the Crisis of Suicide," Public Affairs Pamphlet No. 406 A. 381 Park Ave., S., New York, NY 10016.

Frederick, Calvin J. "Self-Destructive Behavior

Among Younger Age Groups." U. S. Government Printing Office, Washington, DC 20402.

Frederick, Calvin J. "Suicide, Homicide and Alcoholism among American Indians." National Institute of Mental Health, Rockville, MD 20852.

Shneidman, Edwin S. "How to Prevent Suicide," Public Affairs Pamphlet No. 406. 381 Park Avenue, S., New York, NY 10016.

Journal

Psychiatric Annals, Vol. 6, No. 11, Nov. 1976. Insight Communications, Inc., 501 Madison Ave., New York, NY 10022.